MANCHESTER UNITED – CHAMPIONS AT LAST

ALSO BY TOM TYRRELL

Manchester United – the Religion

The Red Devils' Disciples

The Lancashire Soccer Annual

Piccadilly Radio Soccer Book No. 1

Piccadilly Radio Soccer Book No. 2

Soccer Superstars Annual 1978

Soccer Superstars Annual 1979

Soccer Superstars Annual 1980

Soccer Superstars Annual 1981

Soccer Superstars Annual 1982

Soccer Superstars Annual 1983

LWT World of Sport Book

Manchester United

Official Manchester United Annual

Manchester United – The Official History
(with David Meek)

Bryan Robson Soccer Skills

Bryan Robson Football Book

Official Manchester United Annual

MANCHESTER UNITED
CHAMPIONS AT LAST

THE OFFICIAL STORY

Tom Tyrrell

PARTRIDGE PRESS

LONDON · NEW YORK · TORONTO · SYDNEY · AUCKLAND

TRANSWORLD PUBLISHERS LTD
61–63 Uxbridge Road, London W5 5SA

TRANSWORLD PUBLISHERS (AUSTRALIA) PTY LTD
15–25 Helles Avenue, Moorebank, NSW 2170

TRANSWORLD PUBLISHERS (NZ) LTD
3 William Pickering Drive, Albany, Auckland

Published 1993 by Partridge Press
a division of Transworld Publishers Ltd
Copyright © Tom Tyrrell 1993

A catalogue record for this book is available from the
British Library.
ISBN 185225 226X

.

Typeset in 10½/13pt Palatino by
Chippendale Type Ltd, Otley,
West Yorkshire
Printed in Germany by
Mohndruck Graphische
Betriebe GmbH, Gütersloh

To Manchester United supporters throughout the world who waited so patiently for the great day to come; to Alex and the boys of '93

CONTENTS

CHAPTER ONE

CHAMPIONS AT LAST

I T HAD BEEN RAINING ALL DAY IN MANCHESTER, and for most of the previous twenty-four hours too. It was the kind of weather strangers expect when they visit the city, arriving with the preconception that the place is always under a constant deluge, when nothing could be further from the truth.

The rain had come at the end of two weeks of constant sunshine. It was welcomed by the gardeners, predicted by the cricketers, as they were just starting their season, and ignored by tens of thousands of Manchester United supporters who were ready to cheer their favourites along a ten-mile route as they paraded the Premier League championship trophy.

From mid-afternoon the crowds were gathering in Deansgate – the long shopping street which cuts through the lower end of the city from the cathedral to Knott Mill, where the shops fade away and the street becomes a road once more. There were children wrapped in plastic raincoats; mums and dads draped in flags and scarves; young boys ready to climb to any vantage point rather than bide their time leaning on the miles of crush barriers flanking the road. There were familiar faces – fans who knew one another and who shouted their greetings across the tarmac – and newcomers who hoped to see the United players in the flesh for the first time.

Not for twenty-six years had Manchester seen the championship trophy draped in

United's red and white; this was a special day, and the rain would not spoil it. They stood and they waited. Soaked but contented.

At The Cliff training ground some three miles away they waited too. At first just a handful of supporters huddled outside the big wooden gates, which were guarded by two yellow-jacketed policemen in motor-cycle patrol gear. This was the secret location at which the players would board an open-top bus before their celebration parade began. Secret? By the time the bus left there were hundreds outside.

United had been champions for a fortnight. The season over, Alex Ferguson had become the first manager since the days of Sir Matt Busby to bring the title to Old Trafford. United had finished in style with an amazing game at Wimbledon, which saw Bryan Robson scoring his first Premier League goal. Those three points meant that United had ended their campaign ten clear of second-placed Aston Villa, their rivals till the final run in.

The game at Wimbledon had been an extension to the carnival – which had started in Manchester a week before – with 30,000 crammed into Selhurst Park; the majority of them United followers who treated the match like an Old Trafford fixture. As did Wimbledon, who in tribute to United produced a match programme with a picture of Eric Cantona holding the championship trophy on its front cover.

The euphoria of that closing night in London spilled into the following evening when over 30,000 turned up to watch the first leg of the FA Youth Cup final at Old Trafford. United's youngsters lost to Leeds. The two legs of the final attracted 61,000 – would Old Trafford be big enough to hold the crowds hoping to see the first team in 1993–94?

As the fans waited outside, two open-top buses spewed out diesel fumes in the training-ground car park as their ancient engines ticked over. One bus would head the parade carrying a group of enthusiastic children who were helping to promote Manchester's bid to stage

the Olympic Games in the year 2000; the second bus would carry the players. Fittingly, they would set off in celebration from the place where our journey through the championship season begins.

It was here at The Cliff, after the final training session on the eve of the new season, that Alex Ferguson stood to answer those who claimed United would fail again in 1993 after finishing second to Leeds four months earlier. Some critics said that the disappointment of being so close would have a lasting effect on Ferguson's players, but these were the words of the bitter and envious who expressed their hopes rather than their expectations.

'Everybody is talking about that at present. But we have a good strong squad and they went on a very demanding and exciting run to the finishing tape last season, being involved at the top all the way. That experience will definitely help them.'

Could they overcome the disappointment?

'We shall see. It is all about commitment in the early games. I'm talking about commitment not results. You can't always guarantee yourself a victory but you can judge the appetite and the keenness to play and that will answer all the doubts.'

It has often been said that the League Championship is a marathon, and that the cup competitions are mere sprints. In the League each team plays all the other teams twice and only when the distance has been covered do you know the winner. Like the marathon there are those who sprint away from the gun and exhaust themselves too soon; there are runners who find themselves out in front in strange territory and cannot handle the pressure; and there are those with experience who press steadily on until the finish is in sight. If Alex Ferguson was right, his players had joined the ranks of the experienced, after stumbling close to the tape in the previous race.

The manager's summer-spending had left the fans puzzled. He had not exactly broken the bank, nor had he injected much new blood into the side, despite weeks of newspaper speculation as to who might be pulling on a red shirt as the Premier League began. Dion Dublin was bought from Cambridge to try to end the goal drought, which had plagued the last quarter of the 1991–92 season when in marathon terms United had 'hit the wall'. Dublin had come and as the season began Mark Robins was sold to Norwich City for £800,000. Robins, the dyed-in-the-wool United supporter, was popular with the regulars because of the vital goals he had scored in his brief spells in the first team. And why Dublin and not Alan Shearer?

Stories about the Southampton striker had filled every back page for weeks and the name Manchester United appeared there too. But it seemed that Shearer did not want to play for United and, as that is the vital criterion demanded whenever Alex Ferguson opens negotiations with a player, the deal was never on. Shearer went to Blackburn Rovers whose chairman, Jack Walker, signed a cheque for close on £4 million as Alex Ferguson paid Cambridge £3 million less for Dublin.

Was this a mistake? Only time would tell, but it was rare for Manchester United to find themselves faced not only with a player who seemed reluctant to join them, but with a rival club with the cash to outbid them. Blackburn had ambitions and one of those was to see their name engraved on the trophy at the end of the inaugural season.

As the first day of the season arrived the newspaper experts made their predictions for the championship and United were mentioned by most – not as favourites but as probable contenders. One journal employed an astrologer who saw in the stars that the eventual winners would play in yellow and green. Remember that.

Arsenal, Liverpool and champions Leeds, perhaps Tottenham, and even Nottingham Forest; many of the usual names were there. United had to be included not simply because they had finished second the previous season but because many sports writers had gone on record saying Leeds were 'handed the title'.

The season began at Sheffield United, and it began badly for the Reds, who certainly didn't lack spirit but were short on luck. Injuries and illness hit the squad. Paul Parker, Bryan Robson, Danny Wallace and Neil Webb were unfit; Lee Sharpe was recovering from viral meningitis. The game was exciting, partly because both sides played all out for the whole ninety minutes, but also because during the summer there had been a major change to the rules preventing a kicked back pass to the goalkeeper. This put immediate pressure on 'keepers who lacked any foot control and brought panic from defenders who previously had the soft option of being able to kick the ball back to their own penalty area when under pressure.

'Personally, I'm not afraid of playing the ball with my feet,' was Peter Schmeichel's prematch admission, 'but I think it is a stupid rule. It's a rule that proves that the people who decide this sort of thing don't know the first thing about football. They think this is going to improve the game but I think that it is going to take it to a lower level.'

Only three minutes had gone when there was a mix up in the Sheffield defence. As Sheffield's defenders pondered, Paul Ince made a suicidal lunge at goalkeeper Simon Tracey and joined Ferguson's injured list. Two minutes later he left the field, replaced by Michael Phelan, and by the time Dublin got into the action his new colleagues were trailing 2–1.

'I think we had fourteen strikes at goal this afternoon,' Alex Ferguson said after the game. 'You know that you are going to get these sort of days from time to time and you just have to put them out of your mind.'

Out of sight, but not out of mind, was Mark Robins who that afternoon on his début for Norwich, scored twice against Arsenal, as the Canaries won 4–2 at Highbury, to stun not only the Gunners but the rest of their rivals as well. Was Ferguson's decision to sell Robins going to rebound on him?

Next came Everton and defeat at home. To make matters worse Robins scored again, this time as Norwich beat Chelsea in their first home game. The murmurings in the smart new Press room backstage at Old Trafford were that it was better not to mention this to the manager when he came up to talk about the 3–0 upset!

Fergie took the defeat well but had to wait two more games before the first victory, away to Southampton. Southampton mourned the loss of Shearer, a player who had also scored three times in his opening appearances for Blackburn – who were vying with Norwich for the early leadership as the runners poured away at the start of the marathon.

As if to say 'I told you so,' to those supporters who were questioning the summer dealings, Dion Dublin scored his first goal for United. As it turned out that close-range shot in the dying seconds of the game at The Dell was his only success at first-team level because two games later he was sidelined with a broken leg. The injury came after another away win, 2–0, at Nottingham Forest where there were already signs that Brian Clough's side had lost its way. This was not the Nottingham Forest of old and United could have had many more than those goals from Mark Hughes and Ryan Giggs, which brought a smile back to the faces of those regular supporters dreading the worst so early in the season.

Half-time was approaching in the home clash with Crystal Palace when the ball ran to Dublin in the centre circle. He had his back to the Palace goal as Eric Young came in strongly from behind.

'I felt the force of the tackle and went down. I knew it was a bad one and when Jim McGregor came on I told him that I thought that I had heard a crack,' said Dublin, who was stretchered off to be out of contention for six months. 'I was devastated, just coming to a new club, scoring my first goal and trying to establish myself. It was the last thing I needed.'

United beat Palace with a last-gasp goal from Hughes, and the injury to Dublin reminded supporters of the kind of luck which had followed Neil Webb to Old Trafford – a handful of games then out for months. As for Webb, he

did not seem to figure in Ferguson's plans for this campaign and was the subject of much speculation that his days at the club were running out. This was backed up by the television appearances of Neil's wife Shelly, who made her feelings on the matter quite clear. He was sold back to Nottingham Forest some weeks later.

United marched through September unbeaten, triumphing over Leeds at Old Trafford in a splendid game when Andrei Kanchelskis headed in Giggs's cross, then Steve Bruce booted the ball home after the champions'

(*Left*) Neil Webb took part in just one Premier League game for United before moving back to his former club, Nottingham Forest. Here he supports Darren Ferguson in an effort to stop an Ipswich attack during the game at Old Trafford. © *Empics /Neal Simpson*

(*Below*) The unlucky Dion Dublin receives attention from physio Jim McGregor after the challenge from Crystal Palace's Eric Young left him with a broken leg. Dublin was Alex Ferguson's only signing during the close season of 1992. © *Empics/Neal Simpson*

goalkeeper, John Lukic, had made one of those predictable mistakes while trying to clear under pressure.

There was disappointment in Europe, where in the UEFA Cup they were beaten in a penalty shoot-out in Moscow as darkness descended. No goals in the first leg against Torpedo watched by a paltry 19,998, and then the long trip to Russia where it rained incessantly on the day of the game, as United threw away a lead during the deciding spot kicks.

Five consecutive draws came next during the League campaign. First 1–1 at Tottenham, where Giggs scored a goal which would be replayed for the rest of the season for television audiences. Then against Queens Park Rangers at Old Trafford as memories of a 4–1 débâcle the previous season were erased in a game which failed to produce a goal. The third, at Middlesbrough, was again 1–1 as Steve Bruce saw a penalty rubbed out by a second-half equalizer. For the fourth, the mettle of United was tested by, of all teams, Liverpool. They came to Old Trafford lying in an unusual sixteenth place in the table, but led 2–0 by half-time. United seemed dead and buried, but two

(*Top left*) Champions-to-be versus the reigning champs. Mark Hughes makes his intentions clear during the home clash with Leeds as he holds off a David Batty challenge. United won the game 2–0 as they began their push up the table. © *Action Images*

(*Main picture*) One of the goals of the season as Ryan Giggs rounds Tottenham 'keeper Ian Walker just before half-time in the game at White Hart Lane. It was the United youngster's second strike of the season but Gordon Durie levelled matters eight minutes into the second half. © *Action Images*

(*Below*) It took two late goals from Mark Hughes to save United from defeat in the home clash with Liverpool, who led 2–0 at one stage thanks to goals from Don Hutchison (centre). There is no way through this time as Steve Bruce clears. © *Action Images*

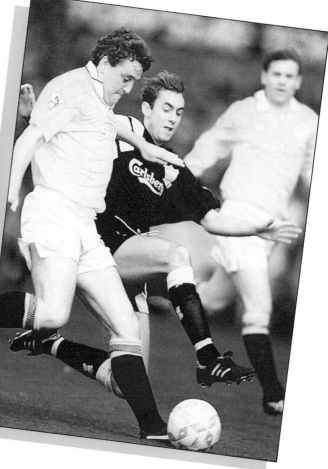

goals from Mark Hughes had the fans scream-
ing and, for the first time in the season, the
signs were there that something might come of
it after all.

The true test would come next. Blackburn
Rovers and Alan Shearer lay in waiting. Since
his record transfer Shearer had paid back Jack
Walker's investment by scoring twelve goals in
as many games, but Blackburn were still
second to Norwich where Robins had scored
half that number. Rovers, though, had beaten
Norwich by an incredible 7–1 scoreline in their

previous home game, so there was a certain
amount of rubbing of hands at the thought of
Manchester United coming to Ewood Park.

The game on Saturday, 24 October failed to
live up to its pre-match billing. Forwards were
cancelled out by defenders. Shearer, who was
anything but popular with the United followers, had a quiet game, and it ended 0–0.
Blackburn went top and stayed there because
the next day Norwich lost 4–1 to Liverpool at
Anfield.

Between them Shearer and Robins had

The Wimbledon fiasco had followed a totally contrasting game at Villa Park in the Coca-Cola Cup which Aston Villa won 1–0, pushing United out of another cup competition, but which – as it had for Leeds a season earlier – may have helped rather than hindered their quest for glory. A week after Wimbledon, Villa did it again, but this time it hurt; a 1–0 loss in Birmingham, three vital points gone.

This was the top of the table on 8 November:

		P	W	D	L	F	A	Pts
1	Arsenal	15	9	2	4	22	13	29
2	Blackburn	15	7	6	2	24	11	27
3	Aston Villa	15	7	6	2	24	15	27
4	Norwich City	14	8	3	3	24	25	27
5	QPR	15	7	5	3	22	15	26
6	Coventry	15	6	5	4	18	18	23
7	Man. City	15	6	4	5	21	14	22
8	Chelsea	15	6	4	5	22	19	22
9	Ipswich	15	4	9	2	20	18	21
10	Man. United	15	5	6	4	14	12	21

As they occupied tenth place, United had not only scored fewer goals than all the sides above them, but only three of the twelve clubs below them – Everton, Southampton and Nottingham Forest – had managed less than fourteen.

'I think that all the talk about the lack of goals at present is taking the confidence out of the side,' Alex Ferguson admitted, 'and when they go behind in a game it has an affect because they know that it will be hard to get back.'

Would it be possible to get back in contention from mid-table? It needed inspiration and that was on the horizon. Oldham Athletic came to Old Trafford and so did the goals. Not one, not two, but three, all for United as they played with the confidence Ferguson spoke

The man who turned his back on United tries to get the better of Gary Pallister. Alan Shearer attacks for Blackburn at Ewood Park but United's defence held the upper hand. © *Action Images*

scored eighteen goals in the Premier League, four more than the total so far achieved by the whole United team. After a dismal game in which they lost 1–0 at home to Wimbledon, it was no surprise when the story got out that Alex Ferguson was on the hunt for a striker. Sheffield Wednesday's David Hirst was the man but all hell broke loose when the news was leaked. Wednesday chairman David Richards refused to listen to any offers United wanted to make, and made it clear that he was not happy to be approached.

about. Two strikes from Brian McClair and Hughes in the space of a minute tilted the game their way and a second from the Scot just short of the half hour and that was that.

Did United really need a new striker? Alex Ferguson thought they did and before the next game he would buy one.

United were due to play Arsenal on Saturday, 28 November and as usual Alex Ferguson had staged his pre-match Press conference on the Thursday lunchtime ready for an early departure the following morning. There was no hint of what was to come. He spoke about the fitness of his players and how he had been able to field what he thought was his strongest side against Oldham, overcoming the disappointment of that defeat at Aston Villa. Arsenal were stiff opposition. Ferguson expected a tough game and United needed to win if they were to keep in touch with the leaders. All straightforward stuff with emphasis on the return of Bryan Robson and Lee Sharpe.

As for all the talk about strikers: 'Well, Brian and Mark will be the first to say they feel better when they are scoring. But sometimes the root of the problem can lie elsewhere and with Lee Sharpe back we could see changes; he is a wonderful crosser of the ball, and Bryan Robson lifts players when he is around.'

By the next morning all those stories were on the spikes of the various sports departments because, at ten minutes to six, just as things were warming up in the daily newspaper offices, came the news that stunned everybody. Eric Cantona had expressed a wish to leave Leeds and Alex had agreed a £1 million deal to bring the Frenchman across the Pennines to Old Trafford. This, according to many who were to look back on United's achievements during the season, was the turning point.

The tall, dark Cantona was at Old Trafford the next morning, going through the routine medical examination before the official signing and in his broken English said: 'I am very happy to be here. If I was not happy I would

not be here. Now together we must win at Manchester United.' The pledge of Eric Cantona.

'It happened quickly,' Alex Ferguson revealed as a hastily arranged Press conference was staged hours after Cantona became one of the United squad. 'And that didn't allow any leaks to come out because you know what this club can be like; no secrets can be kept in this place at all. The clubs agreed on Wednesday night, then the next thing was for Eric to come across and sign.

'I'm delighted. I see Eric as a Manchester United player, the kind of player that we want at this club. He's got style, he's got class, and his goal scoring was instrumental in the success of Leeds last year. So that's why I'm happy to bring another striker to the club, one who has a good reputation and won't in any way be overawed by playing at this club.'

The job done, United set off for London and Arsenal where they won 1–0. Mark Hughes scored as Cantona looked on from the main stand, registered too late to play.

Before leaving the Cantona signing there was a strange twist to the tale. In the Friday morning newspapers Alex Ferguson was being praised for prising Cantona away from Leeds, for whatever reason he had been allowed to leave. Elland Road had been besieged by angry fans for whom Cantona was a cult figure. Cantona was big business for the souvenir shop. They sold more pictures of him than any other player, more T-shirts bearing his name.

The move was compared with United being crazy enough to have sold George Best at the peak of his career, or Liverpool to have parted with Dalglish when he was the inspiration in the side. Yet by Saturday, United had bought a troublemaker: a player who would walk out on them at any second, who was unreliable, and who would demand a first-team place or he would be off. He was someone not to be trusted and had a record which proved this . . . look at the way he had treated Leeds! And he was not that good a player anyway – he had scored only three times as Leeds ran for the

title. How things could change in twenty-four hours.

United fans, however, believed what they saw not what they read. Cantona made his début when he came on as substitute during the derby game against Manchester City at Old Trafford, playing the whole of the second half as Giggs was replaced. His flicks and lobs thrilled, and United won 2–1. He was the same again in the next game, the home clash with Norwich City – who had gone back to the top as Arsenal plunged from first to seventh in three games and United rose to fifth place. Hughes scored this time, Robins had one shot

Mark Hughes and Arsenal's John Jensen tussle for the ball at Highbury. The United striker gave an impressive display scoring the only goal of the afternoon as Eric Cantona looked on from the grandstand. Cantona was signed the previous day, too late to take part in the game. © *Empics/Paul Marriott*

at goal and this was saved by Peter Schmeichel. Alex Ferguson wore a wry smile. The gap narrowed to six points.

Christmas came and went with the signs that this could be United's season after all. A draw at Chelsea; a sensational 3–3 game at Sheffield

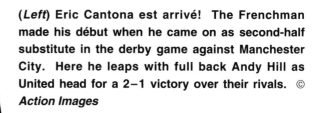

(*Left*) Eric Cantona est arrivé! The Frenchman made his début when he came on as second-half substitute in the derby game against Manchester City. Here he leaps with full back Andy Hill as United head for a 2–1 victory over their rivals. © *Action Images*

(*Below*) Victory over Norwich at Old Trafford gave United three vital championship points and helped them to close the gap on the leaders. Eric Cantona uses his height to win the ball from John Polston as United keep up constant pressure on the Canaries' goal. Mark Hughes scored the winner. © *Action Images*

Wednesday, when United fought back from three down; and then Cantona's first goal in front of his home fans after scoring in both those previous outings. It was United's biggest win since they had beaten Oldham Athletic 6–3 on Boxing Day 1991. United 5 Coventry 0, and remember that Coventry had been one of those early pace-setters who were above United a month before.

United moved into second place and then, after beating Tottenham 4–1, when Cantona got his fourth goal in as many games, they had a taste of life at the top. They were above the rest of the Premier League because of their superior goal difference. What a difference those goals had made. A 3–1 win at Loftus Road and a 2–0 victory over Nottingham Forest at Old Trafford kept them at the top, and

(*Above*) The return of Lee Sharpe made a significant impact on the push for the title. The youngster missed much of the 1991–92 season after a hernia operation and was then seriously ill as the new campaign began. He came back during October and stayed in the side for the remainder of the season. Here he fights for the ball with Chelsea midfielder Graham Stuart during the 1–1 draw at Stamford Bridge. © *Action Images*

(*Right*) It may not have been the goal of the season but it certainly provided one of the most exciting moments as Eric Cantona slips the ball past Sheffield Wednesday 'keeper Chris Woods to equalize at Hillsborough. United fought back from 3–0 down during the Boxing Day game and in the last five minutes came close to winning. © *Action Images*

United had gone ten games without defeat. But then a 2–1 loss at Portman Road to Ipswich, who were making a challenge for the championship themselves, meant a drop to second place.

By February this was how the leaders stood:

	P	W	D	L	F	A	Pts
Norwich City	26	14	6	6	40	38	48
Man. United	26	13	8	5	40	21	47
Aston Villa	26	13	8	5	42	29	47
Ipswich	26	10	12	4	36	29	42
Blackburn	26	11	8	7	39	28	41

Sheffield United were beaten 2–1 at Old Trafford to take United to the top again as they went to Leeds. The reception they got there was frightening. A huge army of Leeds supporters surrounded the team coach as United arrived at Elland Road, and their chants of hatred made it clear that Eric Cantona was far from welcome. 'Scum, scum, scum!' they yelled, beating the side of the bus with their fists, spitting on the United players and on Cantona in particular. There was an equally stormy reception for the players as they walked out to inspect the pitch well before kick-off time, and, throughout the game, whenever the Frenchman touched the ball he was greeted by booing from the very fans who had worshipped his every move only weeks before. Love had turned to hate.

It was a 0–0 draw with Schmeichel denying Leeds their first win over United since they came out of the Second Division. During the game Cantona was booked for using his elbow.

In the next game United were knocked out of the FA Cup at Sheffield United. The result, a 2–1 win for the eventual semi-finalists, is of little importance to our story, but what is of great significance is that that afternoon Manchester United turned the clock back 100 years. They played in a new strip, a jersey first worn

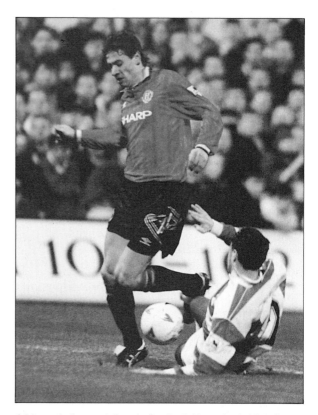

(*Above*) **A goal from Andrei Kanchelskis three minutes into the second half put United 3–1 up against QPR at Loftus Road as the Reds and Aston Villa began their cat-and-mouse run in to the end of the season. Paul Ince and Ryan Giggs got the other United goals that night.** © *Empics/Paul Marriott*

(*Top right*) **Eric Cantona was fined £1,000 for allegedly spitting at a Leeds supporter as he left the field following the 0–0 draw at Elland Road. According to Steve Bruce, Cantona showed remarkable composure throughout his return to his former club. 'They spat at him, threw things at him and hurled abuse in his direction all night.'** © *Empics/Rui Vieira*

(*Right*) **Anfield 1993 and United go top with victory over Liverpool. It is an anxious time for Alex Ferguson and his staff who look on from the bench as goals from Mark Hughes and Brian McClair clinch things. Ian Rush scored a spectacular equalizer for Liverpool early in the second half but McClair's match winner came five minutes later.** © *Action Images*

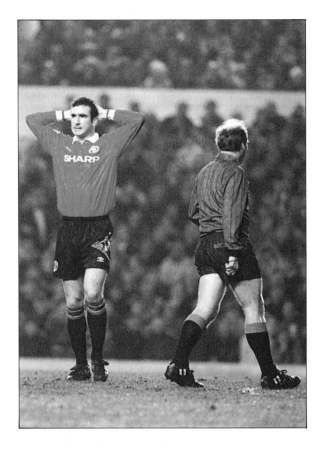

when the club was formed as Newton Heath. It was half green, half gold. What did the astrologer say? Perhaps it was not Norwich after all who would be champions!

A home win over Southampton, then another against Middlesbrough, but United stayed second because new leaders Aston Villa, who were two points in front, had played an extra game. However, there was another booking for Eric Cantona during the Southampton game which sent a shudder through Old Trafford. Just when it looked as if everything was going fine it materialized that Cantona would be suspended for the next two games, both away, at Liverpool and Oldham.

The Anfield game was the usual pressure-cooker football, with United winning 2–1 as McClair and Hughes scored either side of an Ian Rush volley. And so it was off to face struggling Oldham at Boundary Park. Just before the game Ron Atkinson, Villa's manager, stole the headlines in a newspaper article which claimed that United would 'bottle it' again this season, that they would blow up just

24

Paul Parker steals the ball from Aston Villa's Dwight Yorke in the drawn game at Old Trafford. The match was billed as the championship decider but nothing was settled as the game ended 1–1. © *Empics/Ross Kinnaird*

(*Inset*) 'It's my ball.' Peter Schmeichel clears after thwarting a Manchester City attack during the derby game at Maine Road, holding off the challenge of Keith Curle, the Blues' skipper. © *Empics/Barry Coombs*

as the finish was in sight, and that his players would be champions. It was typical Big Ron bravado, but the story grew a little when Oldham beat United, thanks to a Neil Adams goal.

No matter what the Reds did they could not crack the Oldham defence and following the defeat Latics manager, Joe Royle, revealed a conversation he had with Atkinson that morning: 'He told me that he would buy me a bottle of champagne if we beat United and I said if we won I wanted a case not just a bottle.' Joe got his case and the headline writers had a field day: 'Have you got the bottle Fergie?' they asked.

The United manager had made it clear all along that he thought that March would be the toughest month of the season, and it was. As for bottle, he showed no signs of pressure.

Aston Villa themselves had to come to Old Trafford on Sunday, 14 March and the customers

were told this was the championship decider. If it was, nothing was decided, as the game ended 1–1, Hughes rubbing out a Steve Staunton goal with a powerful header. The derby game at Maine Road was a 1–1 draw, then as United drew again at home to Arsenal there was a boost to their hopes. Villa were beaten 1–0 at Norwich, who went back on top, but they had played a game more and were just two points clear of United who had slipped to third.

United's next game? Away to Norwich. The club airlifted 300 fans to Carrow Road, and they were joined by thousands who had travelled across country by coach. They got behind the team from the start urging them on and the players responded as Norwich were hit with such speed and skill they had no answer. By the end of the night United were top once more, winning 3–1 and knowing that it could have been more as Giggs, Kanchelskis

and Cantona had plundered the goals within the first twenty-one minutes. Six games to go and what had Steve Bruce said before the trip back to his former club at Carrow Road? 'Seven matches left and if we can win them all we'll be champions, nobody could stop us then.' Little did he know how true his words would be.

Next came Sheffield Wednesday who threatened to spoil Bruce's prediction. They went ahead through a penalty which was awarded by the stand-in referee after the original, Michael Peck from Kendal, had limped off with a pulled muscle. The game went on and on. Scores, then hundreds, began to pour out of Old Trafford, disconsolate that the dream could end in tatters again. Then Steve Bruce scored. Those early leavers did not know what they had missed; many would hardly have had time to switch on the car radio before Bruce headed the winner, six minutes into time added.

'It's not very often that happens to me,' said the delighted skipper after he had learned that Villa had only drawn at home to Coventry, and United were clear leaders. 'I haven't scored for a long time and I was due one, but I never thought that it would happen in those circumstances. We've all got a bit excited and obviously I'm delighted.

'With six minutes left when we were 1–0 down we felt it might be hard to get back in the game, and memories of Nottingham Forest last year came flooding back. It was the same sort of game, a hot day – we didn't really play that well and the opposition were leading. Chris Woods made some good saves and you got the

feeling that we would never score, but we clawed our way back in and won. I don't know how many times we have gone behind in games this season and come back, but it shows that we can fight all the way.'

That spirit which Alex Ferguson had hoped was still there at the start of the season, was quite apparent now. With five games left, it was against Coventry at Highfield Road where a single shot at goal won the game – Denis Irwin after forty minutes with the vital strike. In the next game United walked over Chelsea 3–0. United were four points clear, three games to play, with Aston Villa due to play Manchester City at Villa Park the next day. If City beat Villa . . . if!

The Blues led at half-time but threw the game away as Keith Curle handled and Villa snapped up a penalty and victory. It was tense stuff and Ron Atkinson seemed noticeably anxious as he was picked out by a close-up television camera. His players were twitching too, but we knew that they had the bottle for the run in. Hadn't Ron said so?

Sky Television was getting ready for the title showdown and decided that it would come on the final day of the season. They moved the games involving United, Villa and Norwich to Sunday, 9 May but then, as Norwich faded, pulled them out of the schedules. United would play Wimbledon at Selhurst Park and kick off at the same time as Villa who were away to QPR, all neatly packaged for television. United had other ideas.

Before their closing game at Selhurst Park, United had to go there on Wednesday, 21 April to face Wimbledon's landlords, Crystal Palace. It was a game of crucial significance to the outcome of the season, but four hours before the kick-off, at the team hotel, the manager and his players seemed totally relaxed as they went through the final preparations. No signs of any twitching, no pressure, no lack of bottle.

The same evening, Villa were away to Blackburn Rovers in a game which kicked off earlier than United's. Even before Steve Bruce led the side onto the pitch the unbelievable news was

Steve Bruce (hidden left) heads home one of the most crucial goals of the season as he scores an injury-time winner against Sheffield Wednesday at Old Trafford. Wednesday had led until the eighty-fourth minute when Bruce scored his first. Then, as the referee added six minutes for stoppages, he ran onto a pass from Gary Pallister to head past England 'keeper Chris Woods. © Action Images

(*Below*) It was United's only clear shot at goal all afternoon, but this Denis Irwin drive was enough to give them victory over Coventry City at Highfield Road. The game gave United their third successive win as they held on to top spot with four matches remaining. © *Action Images*

An aerial battle between Mark Hughes and Chelsea full back Frank Sinclair as United push towards their 3–0 win at Old Trafford. Hughes was on target in the twenty-fifth minute when he forced home a Sharpe cross for his fourteenth Premier League goal. © *Empics/Phil O'Brien*

filtering through from Ewood Park that Blackburn had gone ahead 1–0 then 2. Supporters close to the radio commentary positions were told and passed the news on. The crowd rumbled in anticipation. Sportswriters in the seats in front of the radio positions spent more time trying to hear what the commentators were saying than they did watching the early minutes of the game they were supposed to be covering.

'Still no score here at Selhurst Park . . . but we've just heard some sensational news from up at Blackburn . . . what about this for a scoreline, it's now Blackburn 3 Aston Villa 0.'

Blackburn won 3–0 and, as the crowd urged United on, first Hughes and then Ince got on the scoresheet and the fans who once had hailed Ron Atkinson a hero taunted him across the miles with:

> Are you watching big fat Ron?
> Is it true your bottle's gone?

United played in green and gold that night.

Afterwards Alex Ferguson said calmly: 'We have got ourselves in a fantastic position, two games left and four points clear and a far superior goal difference. There is no way that Villa can catch us on goals. Now we need to do the job properly and it would be lovely to win the championship at Old Trafford for a support that has waited so long. Now hopefully their patience is going to be rewarded.'

The game had been played in front of a crowd of 30,115 at Crystal Palace, while a further 15,000 watched the action on a giant screen at Old Trafford; thousands more had been unable to get in. 'There'll be 50,000 locked out when we play Blackburn,' Alex predicted.

The United manager said that he had heard the scoreline at Ewood Park as he was taking his seat before the kick-off: 'I couldn't believe it when a lad told me it was 2–0, and then somebody said it had gone to 3–0 and at that point I wanted to go down to the pitch and get the players in at half-time because the game was dead. Once they knew the result from Blackburn

they relaxed more and in the second half showed more patience and we deserved to win.'

The Mark Hughes shot from a Cantona cross was the 100th League goal for the Welshman, the second time he had reached a century in a special game. In the 1991 European Cupwinners' Cup Final Hughes had netted the team's 100th of that season.

So the stage was set for the championship decider on Monday, 3 May when Blackburn would be at Old Trafford. But on the afternoon before, Nicky Henry of Oldham Athletic scored. His goal was a lifeline for Oldham, who fought successfully against relegation. It was against Ron Atkinson's side. The final score . . . Aston Villa 0 Oldham 1. The twenty-six-year wait was over.

Two weeks later the crowds outside the training ground got their first glimpse of the players as the open-top bus pulled away flanked by police outriders. Like the supporters, the players ignored the rain as they boarded the top deck exposed to the elements, their only protection baseball caps and thin polythene capes which kept out some of the rain. Water dripped through to the lower deck as the trophy was carried upstairs, and as the journey began Bobby Charlton said: 'The players are delighted to do this sort of thing because winning the championship means so much to the people of Manchester and Salford.

'This is a unique club with a unique following. There is a sort of bond between the club and its supporters which is different here to anywhere else. Other clubs have successes but when you are successful at Manchester United it means so much more. The players and the manager have done a superb job this season. It's been a long wait but it's been worth it.'

People were everywhere, hanging out of windows, standing on the top of telephone kiosks, gathered in huge numbers under bridges where there was some shelter. 'Ooh, aah, Cantona,' they chanted as the Frenchman waved, and one by one the players acknowledged the shouts of the crowd as they were singled out. Deafened by the cheering they enjoyed their journey through the city centre and out into the suburbs to the chant of 'Champions' all the way.

Through Deansgate police walked alongside the bus as their colleagues on horseback held back a sea of followers. The bus passed close to Old Trafford and out through Stretford, Sale and Altrincham at around ten miles an hour. As it reached the end of the route the players descended to the shelter of the lower deck to be carried off to their assembly point.

Rain-soaked, but happy, they waved to the last of the supporters. An estimated half a million had waited for hours in the rain. A longer wait was over now and Manchester United were champions.

Mark Hughes brushes aside the attentions of Andy Thorn as he attacks Crystal Palace at Selhurst Park. 'Sparky's' goal in the sixty-fourth minute was his 100th in the League and it was followed by a Paul Ince shot two minutes from time as the championship celebrations began. United were four points clear of the field with two games to play. © *Action Images*

Sir Matt Busby was a man of vision and saw European competition as the pinnacle of the game. His side reached that goal in 1968 when they became the first English club to win the Champions Cup. Under Sir Matt, United won the First Division five times, – in 1952, 1956, 1957, 1965 and 1967. © *Empics*

CHASING THE DREAM

N THE SUMMER OF 1991, BOBBY CHARLTON WAS standing in the gangway of the Directors' Box at Old Trafford, looking out on the stadium where improvement work was being carried out. The terraces were empty. Facing him in what nowadays is the North Stand, but was once United Road, giant letters formed by white seats set against red spelled the word 'U-N-I-T-E-D'. 'They call this the Theatre of Dreams, and you only have to take a look at it to understand why . . . '

The man who remains Britain's best-known footballer, long after the years when he pulled on the red shirt of United or the white of England, has played a part in those dreams, and no-one would argue that, even when it is deserted, there is an atmosphere of awe and grandeur about the United stadium.

A cantilever roof encircles the perimeter and thousands of red seats form a glistening background, focusing the eyes on the playing area, scene of triumph, tragedy, drama and despair in its eighty-three-year history. Looking out on that arena it is easy to dream and to conjure up visions of vast crowds of chanting, cheering football followers urging on their heroes; of great goals scored by the mighty men who have played both for and against United in the years since Old Trafford was conceived by the fertile imagination of a Victorian footballing giant.

The club itself was created from simple

roots. It began as a leisure pursuit of a group of engine drivers and their colleagues in the sheds off the Oldham Road. Newton Heath is a district of Manchester, just two miles outside the city centre, and the workers named their side after their depot – Newton Heath LYR (Lancashire and Yorkshire Railway Company). They played in green and gold at grounds in North Road, Monsall, then later Bank Street, Clayton, by which time links with the railway company had faded. In 1892 Newton Heath became members of the Football League, elected to an extended First Division. But ten years later the club found itself on the verge of bankruptcy.

The emergence of Manchester United is well documented and it is remarkable that what today is possibly the world's best known football club was created purely by chance. The key was a St Bernard dog owned by Harry Stafford, player and backbone of Newton Heath, which wandered away from a bazaar being held in the city centre to raise much needed cash for the struggling club. The dog was given shelter by a local publican. Somehow John Henry Davies, the imposing owner of Manchester Breweries Ltd, found out about the dog, either on a visit to the pub which belonged to his company, or from the landlord himself.

How matters not. What was important was the bringing together of Stafford and Davies when the latter expressed his wish to buy the dog as a present for his daughter. It gave Stafford the chance to tell Davies of Newton Heath's plight, and led to him gathering together a group of business acquaintances who eventually took control of the club. Newton Heath sank, Manchester United rose to the surface, and Davies and Stafford found their place in history.

Davies then appointed Ernest Mangnall as secretary-manager and from that moment the club never looked back. Mangnall was the first man of vision to take the helm of Manchester United and no-one could argue that Matt Busby came next and then Alex Ferguson,

even though almost a century separates first from third.

Together Mangnall and Davies planned a revolutionary new stadium in an area on the opposite side of the city to Newton Heath's birthplace. It was built on land skirting the Manchester Ship Canal, alongside a railway and within walking distance of the tram terminal. The ground was a concrete bowl, terraced for most of its circumference, with the exception of a small covered grandstand on the railway side where dignitaries and club officials could sit in shelter while the masses braved the elements. This was Old Trafford.

The Theatre of Dreams opened in 1910, two years after the club won its first League Championship and twelve months after United beat Bristol City to win their first FA Cup. A year after its opening the stadium saw its first championship celebrations as United topped the League in 1911. Billy Meredith was the inspiration in the side, a legendary player who had spells with both Manchester clubs. As did Ernest Mangnall, for after his work in the creation of Old Trafford, the manager later moved to City where he helped in the planning and building of Maine Road.

The championship campaign of 1911 ended:

	P	W	D	L	F	A	Pts
Man. United	38	22	8	8	72	40	52
Aston Villa	38	22	7	9	69	41	51
Sunderland	38	15	15	8	67	48	45
(Note: Two points for a win)							

It was three decades later before another man of vision came to the club. The years between saw the ebb and flow of Manchester United's fortunes both on and off the field. They were relegated to the Second Division three times, spending seven seasons there, emerging twice as runners up, and once, in 1936, as champions. The trophy in 1936 was the club's first recognizable honour for a quarter of a century. Hardly the stuff from which dreams are made!

During the bleak 1930s, the club came close to slipping into the Third Division and closer still to going out of business altogether until another major benefactor produced a well-timed cheque book. This was James Gibson, owner of a textile company which made army uniforms. In the years between two World Wars it was no surprise that Gibson had the capital to invest in the club. He paid players' wages when there was no cash to spare, and during the years when the game was suspended because of the Second World War, he helped plan the appointment of Matt Busby.

Busby took over Ernest Mangnall's dream, but found it in ruins. Old Trafford was hit by German bombs during a misdirected air raid on Manchester Docks. Like Mangnall, Busby had not only to rebuild his team, but his stadium as well. Matt Busby was a man of true vision. He chased not one dream but many. He saw club football as a game to be played far beyond the reaches of the League. Busby dreamt of Europe. First he had to create a side capable of competing with the best on the domestic level, then he would reach for his next goal.

His first successful side included Johnny Carey, Stan Pearson and Jack Rowley and won the FA Cup in 1948 – something no United manager had done since Ernest Mangnall. His Red Devils captured the imagination of the football supporters hungry for the game again after the virtual famine of the War Years. Busby's side won the cup in style, beating Liverpool 3–0, Charlton 2–0, Preston 4–1 and Derby 3–1, before a 4–2 victory over Blackpool at Wembley. United played every round away from Old Trafford which was still under repair. (In 1990 when Alex Ferguson's side won the FA Cup they followed a similar path to Wembley after being drawn away from home for each round.)

In 1952, two years after that cup win, Manchester United were champions after the bitter disappointment of being runners-up the previous season, again a pattern which fate would repeat later in the club's history. United had taken second place in 1947, 1948 and 1949. Supporters at that time could have been forgiven for thinking that the title might never return to Old Trafford, just as their successors did between 1967 and 1993. But in 1952 the Championship Trophy was proudly hoisted by Matt Busby and his players in the Theatre of Dreams.

The season ended:

	P	W	D	L	F	A	Pts
Man. United	42	23	11	8	95	52	57
Tottenham H.	42	22	9	11	76	51	53
Arsenal	42	21	11	10	80	61	53

Busby was far from finished. With his assistant Jimmy Murphy, a man who lived for football, he had planned a youth structure at the club which saw the emergence of a team of teenage players which captured the hearts of all who saw them. They played fast, attacking football, always looking for goals. They excited the supporters to such an extent that vast numbers turned up to watch them play. The Football Association introduced a new competition for junior players and for the first five years Manchester United dominated the FA Youth Cup collecting the trophy every year from 1953 until 1957. Is it any wonder that the Busby Babes became a legend?

The manager realized that time was running out for his 1948 side and started to inject new blood from the youth team. Roger Byrne, Jackie Blanchflower, Mark Jones and Geoff Whitefoot began the transformation, forcing out established names. It was a football revolution. The average age of the side dropped drastically as older men gave way to teenagers and players in their early twenties. Crowds flooded to see the Babes, and in 1956 they were such a formidable force that they swept to the championship well clear of the field:

	P	W	D	L	F	A	Pts
Man. United	42	25	10	7	83	51	60
Blackpool	42	20	9	13	86	62	49
Wolves	42	20	9	13	89	65	49

The championship provided the ambitious Busby with the key he needed to open the door to his dream . . . European success for his young players. England was already a step behind the Continent where in 1955 a tournament had been launched which demanded as its qualifying edict that contestants were champions of their domestic league. Busby travelled to Spain to see the new competition as Real Madrid performed before vast audiences in the city's Bernabau Stadium against sides like Partizan Belgrade – the Yugoslav champions who brought to Madrid a contrasting style of football. He saw his dream before him, and he wanted it for Manchester United.

'It was the true test for a football team, the chance to see how good you really were. To be the best, you had to play against the best and the challenge lay beyond our shores. We had to play in Europe on a regular basis, to open up the game and see what it had to offer,' he said.

Thirty years ahead of his time Matt Busby had visions of a European League. Football's hierarchy was unmoved. When he asked for permission to take his side into the European Cup he was refused. So Manchester United ignored the pending wrath of the Football Association, entered the competition in its second year, and Busby's young champions reached the semi-final before losing to Real Madrid.

On the way, they had slaughtered Belgium's top club, Anderlecht, in a 10–0 second-leg game, played at Maine Road because at the time Old Trafford was without floodlights; and Busby brought teams like Borussia Dortmund and Atletico Bilbao to Manchester to be viewed by the curious. European football was an immense success.

The Babes were such a force in the English game that it was no surprise when they were crowned champions once more in 1957. Victory again was clear cut:

	P	W	D	L	F	A	Pts
Man. United	42	28	8	6	103	54	64
Tottenham H.	42	22	12	8	104	56	56
Preston	42	23	10	9	84	56	56

The Babes also reached the FA Cup Final of 1957, but the elusive League and Cup 'double' eluded them when they lost 2–1 to Aston Villa at Wembley.

A year later, on 6 February 1958, Matt Busby's dream was shattered. The team was returning in triumph from a European Cup tie against Red Star Belgrade when the aircraft carrying the Babes, club officials and some of the country's top journalists, crashed after refuelling at Munich.

Eight players died, two more had their careers cut short by the injuries they sustained, and as many sportswriters perished, amongst them Frank Swift, the former England goalkeeper who had played his football for United's rivals Manchester City. Busby himself was badly injured: 'I wanted to turn my back on the game but my dear wife, Jean, said that I owed it to those boys who had died to continue.'

His dream was to win the European Cup as a lasting memory to the Babes. Led by Jimmy Murphy, as Busby recovered his health, United's makeshift side, made up of survivors, young reserves and players brought to Old Trafford after the League waived the transfer deadline, again reached the semi-final of the European Cup, but lost to AC Milan. They got to Wembley but were beaten by Bolton Wanderers in the FA Cup Final. They slipped to ninth in the League, winning just one First Division game after the crash when before it they had been favourites to retain the title for a third season. A wave of sympathy engulfed

The last line-up. The most poignant picture in the history of Manchester United as the Busby Babes prepare to face Red Star Belgrade in Yugoslavia. Twenty-four hours later the Munich Air Disaster took twenty-three lives, including those of eight players and four club officials. *Left to right*: **Duncan Edwards, Eddie Colman, Mark Jones, Ken Morgans, Bobby Charlton, Dennis Viollet, Tommy Taylor, Bill Foulkes, Harry Gregg, Albert Scanlon and Roger Byrne.**

the club, enlarging United's already immense and nationwide support.

They were offered the chance to play in Europe once again in the season following the disaster but rejected the invitation. If United were to play in the Champions' Cup they would do so as champions. Matt Busby vowed to return to the top and incredibly, urged on by massive support, United were runners-up in 1959 in a season when Dennis Viollet set a new record by scoring thirty-two League goals – a peak which to this day has not been surpassed.

In the next four seasons the highest League position they could achieve was seventh, but five years after Munich the new generation brought its first success to Old Trafford. Threatened at one stage with relegation, they battled their way to Wembley to win the 1963 FA Cup Final by beating Leicester City 3–1. Scorer of six goals in that campaign, including one in the final, was Denis Law, a key figure in the success which was to follow. He was bought from Italian club Torino for a record fee at the time of £115,000 after moving there from Manchester City.

Law's career began at Huddersfield Town under the managerial eye of Bill Shankly. During his first season at Old Trafford he was joined by another Scot as Pat Crerand, an international wing-half, moved from Glasgow Celtic to link up with Munich survivor Bill Foulkes and local youngster Nobby Stiles to form United's midfield. Bobby Charlton, who as a twenty-year-old had lived through the air

United's first success after Munich as they pick up the FA Cup after beating Leicester City 3–1 at Wembley. *Left to right*: Tony Dunne, Bobby Charlton, Noel Cantwell, Pat Crerand, Albert Quixall, David Herd and Johnny Giles. *Action Images/Football Association*

crash, had emerged as one of England's most outstanding players, and in the season following that cup success he and Law were joined by a young player who had been unearthed by the club's scouting system in Northern Ireland . . . George Best.

Law, Best and Charlton played together for the first time at The Hawthorns on 18 January, 1964, when West Brom were beaten 4–1. All three scored, Law twice.

United were in contention for the title for most of the season, but dropped vital points during March and saw the championship slip from their grasp when they lost to the eventual winners, Shankly's Liverpool, at Anfield. But it was only a matter of time before the new United reached the top. They were an inspirational side and in Best they possessed a player who ranked amongst the all-time greats.

In 1965, for the first time since the days of The Babes, Manchester United were crowned champions. They won by the narrowest of margins, beating Don Revie's Leeds United on goal average, winning by just 0.69 of a goal. At that time, the method used for separating teams level on points was to work out the average number of goals scored by dividing goals 'for' by those 'against'. United had netted 89 and conceded 39 (2.28), while Leeds scored 83 and conceded 52 (1.59). (Today's system of 'goal difference' would have put United well ahead with a +19 advantage).

With two points for a win the 1965 title race ended:

	P	W	D	L	F	A	Pts
Man. United	42	26	9	7	89	39	61
Leeds Utd	42	26	9	7	83	52	61
Chelsea	42	24	8	10	89	54	56

Leeds and Liverpool, who emerged from the Second Division in 1962, were the biggest threats to Busby's new United but once again the United manager had the chance to reach for European glory and in 1966 came close to achieving his aim. For a third time United reached the semi-finals of the European Cup but again they stumbled.

In the quarter-final stages George Best had perhaps his finest game when, virtually single-handed, he destroyed the might of Benfica in Lisbon. After a narrow 3–2 win at Old Trafford in the first leg, United ran rampant through the Portuguese on their own soil, taking the second game 5–1 with Best scoring twice. United were then drawn against Yugoslav club Partizan and had to return to Belgrade, a city full of sad memories. They lost 2–0, and although they won the return leg 1–0, glory slipped from their grasp.

It was after that game that Pat Crerand made Busby a promise. 'He told me that we would win the championship again the following season and go on to win the European Cup. He was trying to soften the blow of the disappointment of defeat after getting so far in the competition. I thought to myself if ever there was the eternal optimist then here he was!'

Optimist or not, Crerand was right. In 1966–67 United won the championship and in 1968 they became the first English holders of the European Cup, beating Benfica at Wembley in a marvellous final. Matt Busby had fulfilled his ultimate dream; he had won Europe's biggest prize. Busby saw it as a tribute to those players who had given everything trying to reach his goal ten years earlier. Now he felt it was time to stand aside and make way for a new man to guide United to future glories.

But at this point let us pause. For more than two decades United had dominated football at a time when the balance of power in the game was spread amongst a group of at least ten clubs rather than the élite half dozen of today. Who would imagine that it would be close on thirty years before the championship pennant would once again fly at Old Trafford, and by which time the leading characters in those glory days of the Sixties would have long given up playing?

This is where Pat Crerand comes into our story once more. The craggy Scottish half-back has an immense affection for United and he makes it obvious to anyone who talks to him. His love for Manchester is such that when his playing days ended he did not return to his native Scotland but like Denis Law continued to live in the area. His home is a short drive from the Theatre of Dreams.

'If anyone had said to me, after we won the championship in 1967, that Manchester United would not win it again in the next quarter of a century, I would have told him he was mad. We were the best team in the Europe and it was only a matter of time before we won the title again.'

How true. But the unbelievable happened. When Old Trafford staged the 1967 parade of England's top trophy, not one supporter in that joyful crowd of 61,071 watching a sun-drenched lap of honour by Matt Busby and his players realized they were witnessing the end of an era. Who would have guessed as the Stretford Enders chanted 'We are the champions!', while player after player was handed the trophy to hold above his head, that the name of Manchester United would never again be engraved upon it?

Sir Matt's fifth championship, but it saw the start of a twenty-six-year wait before the title returned to Old Trafford. The 1967 side clinched the First Division when they beat West Ham at Upton Park a week before the trophy was paraded before the closing game of the 1966–67 season. ©
Syndication International

Who could dream that by the time United were again crowned champions it would be not of the First Division, but of a new Premier League run by the Football Association; that players would move from club to club for millions; that it would cost more to watch a game than those supporters earned in a week; and that the famous Stretford End would itself have given way to progress and become the all-seater 'West Stand'? No astrologer could have kept their credibility had they been reckless enough to make such outrageous predictions.

At regular intervals United had been crowned champions. It was not a divine right, but a fact of life. They won in 1952, 1956, 1957, 1965, 1967. Why doubt that this pattern should not continue during the Seventies and Eighties? In the crowd of 1967 were many supporters who had been present at previous presentations. They would have applauded and cheered just as loudly as Duncan Edwards, Roger Byrne and Tommy Taylor stood alongside their manager, as they did when Busby was flanked by Denis Law, George Best and Bobby Charlton.

Yet the youngsters who saluted their heroes as they paraded in 1967 would have children of their own before Old Trafford witnessed such a scene again. Those mini-skirted girls, attracted to football by the pop-star image of George Best, would be middle-aged women; the Beatle-cropped youths would be balding grandfathers. Many would not even live to see the day.

The 1966–67 championship campaign had started well with wins over West Bromwich Albion at Old Trafford, and Everton at Goodison Park. But a 3–1 defeat by Leeds at Elland Road stunned players and supporters alike. They saw the result as a clear indication that the rivals of 1965 would again haunt United's title ambitions. It was no great surprise either when Leeds took a point in the return fixture at Old Trafford on the final day of 1966.

On Boxing Day, United had lost to Sheffield United at Bramall Lane in a game which proved significant as their last defeat of the season. Busby's team then went on to the top after playing twenty games without losing. But it was how they took the title which thrilled everyone.

After beating Aston Villa 3–1 at Old Trafford, the last away game of the season was at Upton Park, where England's World Cup heroes – Bobby Moore, Geoff Hurst and Martin Peters – stood between United and success. West Ham were a force to be reckoned with despite their mid-table position, but United ignored their threat and ran the Hammers into the ground. An army of supporters went frantic with delight as two goals from Law, and others from Best, Charlton, Crerand and Foulkes, gave United a 6–1 victory. On the final whistle the fans flooded onto the pitch to form a sea of hair, hands and smiling faces in front of West Ham's main stand chanting 'Champions, champions,' and clapping out a samba rhythm. They refused to leave until Busby and his jubilant players appeared.

Thousands who were not in London that day had turned up at Old Trafford a week later to witness the trophy presentation. A year on, many of those same supporters were at Wembley to see the European Cup final before packing the streets of Manchester as United returned in triumph.

Then came the transition. In their European Cup winning season United ended their League campaign in second place, two points behind Manchester City, but there were signs that the Sixties team could not go on for much longer. A mere seven League wins between August and Christmas 1968 was an indication that all was not well, and early in the New

The players who formed the backbone to Sir Matt Busby's dream team of the Sixties. George Best, Bobby Charlton, and Denis Law carried United to the championships of 1965 and 1967 and their skills were recognized throughout the world. Here George Best receives the European Footballer of the Year award from his manager as two previous winners look on during a unique occasion. © Oldham Chronicle

Year, when Sir Matt decided to 'go upstairs', there were those who predicted that the new man would have to make drastic changes to an ageing side.

The club's most successful manager decided that his future was to be in the role of general manager, leaving team affairs in the hands of Wilf McGuinness, one of the Babes whose playing career was badly hit by injury. It was through injury that McGuinness was not included in the Munich party. He was left behind in his native Manchester, while his best friend and room-mate Duncan Edwards flew out to Belgrade with the rest of the team and was one of the eight players who died.

'When I was a youngster Wolves wanted to sign me and they were the top team at the time, but once I'd met the great man and Jimmy Murphy that was that. I was United daft anyway and didn't need much persuasion,' said McGuinness.

With Busby on hand to advise him, McGuinness handled team affairs until the summer of 1969 when he was officially made manager. In his first few months United stuttered along ending the season in eleventh place. He improved this by three positions the following season, with his most remarkable achievement being a 4–1 win over Liverpool at Anfield. But by December 1970, McGuinness was back in charge of United's reserve side.

The Board had been prepared to take a backseat as McGuinness was given the chance to prove himself, but they decided that the role of manager should go to a more experienced man, especially as the club wanted to continue its success of the previous two decades. While they looked for that man, Sir Matt once more took over amid rumblings that personality clashes had caused problems in the dressing room.

The summer of 1971 saw Frank O'Farrell appointed. Before the new man arrived United had been eighth in the League for two successive seasons. In 1972 the former Leicester City manager guided them to exactly the same position, despite having the advantage of leading the table, five points clear, at one stage in the season. He had problems with George Best, who walked out on the club for a period, but in Martin Buchan he signed a player who would have an important role in future successes. O'Farrell chased the dream and fell well short. In December 1972 after just eighteen months as manager he was sacked.

His dismissal followed a spectacular defeat at, of all places, Selhurst Park, where the 1993 campaign was to take such a significant turn. United, in a bad way with just five victories in the first half of the season, were far from safe as they were thrashed 5–0 by Crystal Palace. Watching that defeat on Saturday, 16 December 1972, was the man who would succeed O'Farrell, Thomas Henderson Docherty. By the next game The Doc was United's manager and O'Farrell was suing for compensation.

Docherty became a fans' manager. They saw in him someone who was able to relate to the terraces and handle himself in the boardroom. His ebullient style lifted the gloom from United immediately, but his rapierlike tongue impaled its victims with rapid regularity. First to suffer was Ted MacDougall, a prolific scorer with his previous clubs who had been bought by O'Farrell for a record fee. 'He can't play football,' was Docherty's assessment.

United ended the 1972–73 season in eighteenth place, avoiding relegation, but only just. A season later, as Docherty tried desperately to right things after buying Lou Macari, Jim Holton and George Graham, United went down. In reality the demise of the side had been threatening from as early as 1969, a year in which United again reached the European Cup semi-final and brought South American opposition to Old Trafford as they played Estudiantes of Argentina in the World Club Championship. There were signs that things were not going well but relegation was a jolt to United's system.

If Docherty's dream was to lift the championship and emulate Busby, he now had to get out of the Second Division before he could even consider that aim. Stuart Pearson was

bought from Hull City, Steve Coppell from Tranmere Rovers, and Docherty used twenty-four players in his efforts to get back into the top section. His scheme worked. After just one season in Division Two, United returned as champions. While it was impossible to compare this success with that of taking the League title, they were at least going in the right direction.

At the end of the following season the supporters were flooding in to see an exciting United side which still had Alex Stepney in goal – the last of Busby's players, and the one remaining link with 1968. Best had gone, later revealing that drink problems had led to his many walk-outs; Bobby Charlton had retired; Denis Law had moved to Manchester City, where he played a part in United's demise with his back-heeled goal at Old Trafford which, while not sending United down as many have since said, certainly made their chances of surviving relegation extremely difficult; European Cup Final goal-scorer Brian Kidd was sold to Arsenal, and Sammy McIlroy – who

Wilf McGuinness was the man with the unenviable task of succeeding Sir Matt Busby and his reign as manager was short. He is seen here with Busby and (*far right*) the then chairman Louis Edwards, late father of United's present chief executive Martin Edwards. While Sir Matt dreamt of glory in Europe, Louis Edwards had a vision of Old Trafford one day becoming the finest stadium in the country. Many would say that goal was reached in 1993. *Syndication International*

was signed by United when Matt Busby was manager – made his début under Docherty.

United ended the season in third place, their highest position since 1968. They got to Wembley for their first FA Cup final since 1963, but lost 1–0 to Southampton. With a Crerand-like prediction Martin Buchan pledged to return. A season later, after United achieved sixth place in the League, Buchan became the first player to collect both the English and Scottish FA cups after captaining United to their 2–1 win over Liverpool.

George Best at his best. The Irish imp leaves an opponent sprawling as he jinks his way towards goal. Best was a remarkable player who won the hearts of United supporters during the Sixties. However, drink was his downfall and his career ended amid confusion and controversy. Today George is in demand once again as a radio and television personality and his popularity has never waned. © *Author*

Bobby Charlton played a record 606 League games for United as well as making 106 appearances for England. He won championship medals in 1957, 1965 and 1967, was a member of the FA Cup winning side of 1963, and skipper of the side which won the European Cup in 1968. Today he is a director of the club and is known throughout the world as a great ambassador for the game. *Action Images/Football Association*

It was to be Tommy Docherty's finest and final hour. There could be no questioning his achievements at the club, a vibrant side with exciting players who could challenge for success, and yet there had been undercurrents for some time that all was not well. Before reaching Wembley Docherty had threatened to resign for reasons known only to himself. As Manchester celebrated the cup win he revealed that for some time he had been having an affair with the wife of the club's physiotherapist Laurie Brown. It was a subject far removed from football, but it was given as the reason for Docherty to be dismissed. In the summer of 1977 as Docherty set up home with Mary Brown – who today is Mrs Mary Docherty, mother of his two lovely daughters – United appointed Dave Sexton as the next man to chase the dream.

Wilf McGuinness, Frank O'Farrell, Tommy Docherty, and now Queen's Park Rangers' manager Sexton, who like Docherty had been in charge of Chelsea. Each succeeded Sir Matt and each in turn found it an impossible act to follow. Outsiders said that Busby's influence was still there, that the fact he had an office at Old Trafford meant that he was looking over the shoulder of the manager, adding to the pressure of the job. Docherty dismissed this. 'Sir Matt was there a lot. He used to come to the club every day, but only to have lunch with his pal Jimmy Murphy who did a bit of scouting after he retired or to have a chat with the other people he knew. He never interfered, but if you wanted any advice you could always turn to him.'

Docherty and Sexton were contrasting characters. While the Doc was a showman, Sexton was quiet and deep thinking, a man who would spend his spare time reading, adding to his knowledge of a wide variety of subjects which had nothing to do with the game. As for his ability as a manager, it was not in question. He was a brilliant coach, who graduated from West Ham's 'academy'. But Sexton was an introvert and found it difficult to communicate with the supporters in the way Docherty had,

Tommy Docherty breezed into Old Trafford and left in a storm. The jovial Scot won the FA Cup in 1977, but he will always be reminded that he was in charge when United were relegated in 1974. They spent just one season in Division Two, the only time they have been out of the top section in more than fifty years. © *Empics*

by capturing their hearts with regular appearances on television and radio. Docherty made headlines, Sexton avoided them.

'I'm not one to help people fly kites,' he said after newspapers speculated that he was about to plunge into the transfer market. 'If they want to play guessing games they can get on with it.' Docherty would have confirmed or denied the rumours, or given the media a different path to follow. He had a knack of being able to say anything about anything, while Sexton preferred to say nothing.

In Sexton's first season United finished

tenth, with their defence bolstered by the addition of Gordon McQueen. He was bought from Leeds United, and followed his close friend and Elland Road team-mate Joe Jordan to Old Trafford as Sexton made his intentions clear. He wanted to become the first man since Busby to lift that championship trophy for Manchester United.

In 1978–79 Sexton's side still had much of Docherty's influence about it and improved on the previous term by just one place . . . ninth was a long way from the title. United did get back to Wembley, but lost to Arsenal in the famous 'five minute final'. The London club seemed to have tied up the match with only a few minutes remaining when United pulled back two goals and then gave away a disappointing winner.

In the summer of that year, Sexton signed Ray Wilkins, a player who had been with him at Chelsea, for £850,000. Sexton looked upon Wilkins as the final part of the elusive jig-saw puzzle that managers regard as their perfect side.

In 1980 United were again runners-up in the First Division, losing the championship to Liverpool by just two points. But at the end of the next season Dave Sexton was sacked. 'I must be the only manager to end a season with seven successive wins and still lose his job,' was his comment after taking the club to eighth place.

Ron Atkinson became the fifth man to follow Busby. Aware that he was not first choice having read the newspaper headlines linking Lawrie McMenemy, Bobby Robson and Brian Clough to the post – although not all had been positively offered the chance of taking charge – Atkinson was determined that now he was United's manager, he would manage United. In came Atkinson and out went coaches Harry Gregg, Jack Crompton and Syd Owen, as well as physio Laurie Brown. Crompton and Gregg linked the 1981 side with Busby's post-war team. Crompton had kept goal in the 1948 cup final; Gregg had survived Munich and made appearances in the championship years of 1965 and 1967.

Joe Jordan left to join AC Milan, so Atkinson bought Frank Stapleton from Arsenal and eventually, after prodding and probing in the transfer market for several players, including Trevor Francis, Frank Worthington and Mark Lawrenson, he went back to West Bromwich Albion, his former club, and bought both Bryan Robson and Remi Moses in a deal worth a massive £1.75 million.

In his first season, Atkinson equalled Docherty's League achievements by finishing in third place. He overtook him a year later by not only finishing third once more but also winning the FA Cup in a replayed final at Wembley when Brighton were beaten 4–0.

Norman Whiteside had emerged from the youth team to become the youngest player to appear in the World Cup finals, a record which until 1974 had been held by no less a mortal than Pele. While the team slipped to fourth place by the 1983–84 season another newcomer caught the headlines – Mark Hughes, a robust and highly talented Welsh teenager.

Atkinson took the mantle of United's third most successful manager after Busby and Mangnall, when he won the FA Cup for a second time. The 1985 final was decided by a goal from Whiteside, but the game against Everton is remembered by most because it was the one in which the unfortunate Kevin Moran found his way into the record books by becoming the first player to be sent off at Wembley. Those cup successes, coupled with reasonable progress in Europe – in the Cup-Winners' Cup in 1983–84 United reached the semi-final stage and in 1984–85 they were quarter finalists in the UEFA Cup – gave supporters hope that the chase for the title might end under Ron Atkinson. In 1985 it seemed as if his dream would be fulfilled.

That summer Atkinson had bought Gordon Strachan from Alex Ferguson's club Aberdeen. Strachan made an instant impact as United began the campaign in fine style. He missed the opening game, a 4–0 win over Aston Villa at Old Trafford, but played in the next eight matches, all of them victories, before dislocating

Ron Atkinson left West Bromwich Albion to replace Dave Sexton at United's helm in the summer of 1981. He took the club to third place in his first two seasons winning the FA Cup in 1983 then again in 1985. His teams never finished below fourth place but he failed to land the championship and in November 1986 made way for Alex Ferguson. ©
Empics/Peter Robinson

In Bryan Robson, Ron Atkinson saw the player who could be the key to the championship. He was the most outstanding midfielder in the country and cost United a record £1.5 million when Atkinson bought him from his former club West Bromwich Albion in October 1981. Robson is the first United player to collect the FA Cup three times – 1983, 1985 and 1990, the European Cup-Winners' Cup, the European Super Cup and, of course, the Premier League championship trophy. ©
Empics/Peter Robinson

his shoulder scoring in the 5–1 win at West Bromwich. This was followed by another win at home to Southampton. After ten matches, United were top of the table with a 100 per cent record, the most successful launch to any season in the club's history.

It was November before they suffered their first defeat, going down 1–0 at Sheffield Wednesday. After being top at Christmas, they were slowly overhauled managing only twelve more wins in the remaining thirty-two fixtures. Liverpool took the championship, Everton were second, and United were fourth behind West Ham.

A year later, following the summer departure of the popular Hughes to Barcelona and with his side in nineteenth place, Ron Atkinson was sacked.

Former Glasgow Rangers striker Alex Ferguson shows some of his old skill as he prepares for a United training session. During his seven years at Old Trafford he has established himself as one of the best managers in the game and his record with United is second only to Sir Matt Busby. ©
Empics/Phil O'Brien

ENTER
ALEX FERGUSON

MARTIN EDWARDS AND HIS FELLOW DIRECTORS waited until the day after Guy Fawkes' Night before dismissing Ron Atkinson, and at least avoided an embarrassment of headlines referring to fireworks, bonfires and gunpowder plots. It was inevitable that the change of management would fill the back pages, but the swiftness with which they found a replacement not only softened the attack – Atkinson was popular with the media – but also deflected the spotlight away from the old and onto the new.

Atkinson and his assistant Mick Brown were summoned to Old Trafford just before training was due to start on Thursday, 6 November 1986. They were told that their services were no longer required thirty-six hours after United had been humiliated at The Dell by a Southampton side which won 4–1 in a League Cup replay. Many who saw the game reckoned that United got off lightly!

Even so, Atkinson was stunned: 'I had no indication of what was going to happen. I came in this morning expecting to have a nice five-a-side and some training, but the chairman sent for me and told me reluctantly – I felt reluctantly – that they had decided to dispense with our services because of the results over the last few months. I accept that totally and I don't feel bitter about it. I don't hold any bitterness against the club at all. I honestly feel we had begun to turn the corner. I came here this morning knowing that we are playing Oxford on Saturday and that I had to get out a side capable of winning there. Now someone else has got that responsibility, and whoever it is I sincerely hope they do well.'

It was ironic that seven years later it would be Atkinson who stood between United and that first championship for twenty-six years, but he made his exit bravely, facing a battery of cameras and microphones as the media besieged The Cliff training ground. The following day Alex Ferguson was sitting at his desk.

Ferguson was a man of rich pedigree in Scotland. He was ambitious and knew that his ability had to be tested in the Football League. Why else should he give up his home and the apparent security of life in Aberdeen? Martin Edwards made it abundantly clear what was demanded from the new manager: 'As we always expect from all our managers, we want him to make us the premier club in England and to do that we have to win the First Division championship. That was our aim all through Ron Atkinson's reign and will continue to be our main priority.' Ferguson's mandate was clear.

Speaking for the first time in the office he inherited from the flamboyant Atkinson, Alex Ferguson seemed far removed from the larger-than-life image of his predecessor. During his days at United 'Big Ron' courted the media, sharing jokes over a cup of tea, and challenging them to football matches – his team of old players and local managers against their squad of enthusiastic young journalists, creaking overweight veterans and the odd ex-player.

Atkinson was outspoken, and at times outrageous. On one occasion the national Press, arriving for a pre-match conference, were confronted by the sight of the Manchester United manager sprawled out on a sunbed. His naked torso glistened under the bright light as he outlined his plans for the next game. He gave radio interviews from his bath – at least complying with requests to avoid excess movement because the sound of water splashing during a football interview could prove confusing to the listener. This was Ron Atkinson – no easy act to follow.

When Alex Ferguson was appointed the telephone lines between Scotland and Manchester were hot with stories about the new man. Journalists north of the border gave their advice on how to handle Fergie. There were tales of a fiery temper, his reluctance and caution when dealing with the Press and how he would lay down the rules and how the media would obey. He would tell them when and where he would be available – in sharp contrast to Atkinson whose office door was always open.

Looking out on the training ground Ferguson picked up where his chairman left off: 'I want to bring the championship back to this club. Finishing second or third is no good to us. We have to finish first and that is obviously my aim.'

Brave words for a manager who was inheriting a club in the relegation zone, but Ferguson was an optimist and six months of the season remained: 'We aren't in a desperate position, even this season the League is there to be won. It's no use me coming here and not thinking that every game we play we can win. We have got to attack things. There's a game to be played tomorrow and we have to go out and win it. Tomorrow we have to win.' That, it seemed, would be Alex Ferguson's motto in his quest for new success.

As for Yesterday's Man, Ron Atkinson did win honours at Old Trafford. A measure of his achievements was that, by collecting the FA Cup twice, maintaining a League position of never lower than fourth, and reaching the European Cup-Winners' Cup semi-final in 1984, he had done more than any other manager with the exception of Sir Matt Busby and Ernest Mangnall. Unlike them he did not win the championship. Ferguson knew that that would be the only yardstick by which his time at Old Trafford would be measured.

Manchester United is a far cry from Aberdeen and it did not take the new manager long to realize this. The first thing he had to handle was the media attention. This was very different to Pittodrie. There he had been miles away from the national newspaper bases and his regular contact with them was by telephone. When Aberdeen played one of the Glasgow giants or were involved in a major game he would come face to face with the leading Scottish writers, but Manchester United attracted the attention not just of the staffmen based in the city, but of the 'Number Ones' from London.

'Cough and it makes headlines,' Tommy Docherty would say, 'sneeze and they'll fill the back page!' Manchester is a leading media base. Network television and radio programmes originate from the city, which has, in Piccadilly Radio, the country's most successful independent station outside London. The *Manchester Evening News* has readers who demand daily information about United to satisfy their appetites.

Tommy Docherty had handled the media perfectly. His Jack-the-Lad attitude went down well with the sportswriters and broadcasters. Dave Sexton followed and the door to the office closed. He was a quiet man who hated the spotlight. If the warnings from Scotland were to be believed Alex Ferguson was more like Sexton than the extrovert Docherty and Atkinson. But he filled his new role superbly. Whether he was putting on a brave face, only Alex Ferguson knows, but he bit the bullet and got down to the side of his job he possibly disliked the most. He appeared on radio and television, held regular press conferences with the daily and Sunday newspapers and came over well. He was genuinely warm to supporters, going out of his way to chat and sign autographs.

As far as the team was concerned, he took a calm approach, prepared to see what Atkinson's players could do before introducing his own.

With him from Aberdeen he brought Archie Knox, a solid, square-chinned man with a machine-gun in his mouth. He would rattle out commands in a rich Scottish accent, and his domineering attitude hid a great sense of humour. Archie had been Alex's friend and assistant for many years and continued in this role at Old Trafford.

In that first season United ended in eleventh place but showed signs that there was better to come.

During his first summer in Manchester Alex Ferguson moved into the transfer market and on 1 July 1987 held a double-signing session at Old Trafford where once again the media gathered like flies. Viv Anderson from Arsenal and Brian McClair, the Celtic striker, joined the squad. Anderson cost just £250,000, McClair's fee was kept to £850,000 by a tribunal when Celtic wanted a million or more.

'When I first arrived at this club I felt that I had to give myself time to look at the players I had taken over. I knew that I would eventually make changes and I have gone on record as saying that I need to strengthen at least five positions. I may already have players for those positions and it's up to them to show me that is the case, but if not, then I will find them elsewhere,' said Ferguson.

Brian McClair quickly paid back Ferguson's investment, scoring thirty-one goals in his first season. The new manager was already reaching back to the glory days. Not since the time of George Best had a United player managed to break the twenty-goal barrier in a League campaign, but in his manager's first full season, McClair did just that. He scored twenty-four First Division goals, seventeen in general play and five from penalties. No-one came near him in the scoring records:

	Div 1	FA	LC
McClair	24	2	5
Robson	11	0	0
Whiteside	7	2	1
Strachan	8	0	1
Davenport	5	0	1

Even so United finished runners up, their highest League position for eight years. But it

(*Above*) Alex Ferguson bought Viv Anderson from Arsenal to add experience to his defence, but the former England full back was plagued by injuries during his time at Old Trafford. Eventually in January 1991 he was transferred to Sheffield Wednesday but has remained a close friend of many of the United players and is a regular visitor to the club. © *Empics/Neal Simpson*

(*Main picture*) Alex Ferguson's first major signing, Brian McClair, tussles for the ball with Earl Barrett during the 1990 FA Cup semi-final against Oldham. Three years later the players found themselves in opposing corners once again, Barrett was a member of the Aston Villa side which threatened McClair's title hopes. © *Empics/Phil O'Brien*

BRIAN MCCLAIR
SCOTTISH INTERNATIONAL

POSITION:	Forward
BORN:	8.12.63 Airdrie
HEIGHT:	5ft 9in
WEIGHT:	12st 2lb
JOINED UNITED:	July 1987
PREVIOUS CLUBS:	Aston Villa, Motherwell, Celtic
UNITED DEBUT:	15 August 1987 v Southampton (a)

was cold comfort. The gap behind champions Liverpool seemed vast under the new three points for a win system:

	P	W	D	L	F	A	Pts
Liverpool	40	26	12	2	87	24	90
Man. United	40	23	12	5	71	38	81

During that campaign, recurring injuries to Paul McGrath led to the signing of Steve Bruce from Norwich for a further £800,000. A twist of fate played its part in the arrival of the player who would have great influence on the future of the club. United were about to sign England centre half Terry Butcher when he broke his leg during a game for Glasgow Rangers. Norwich demanded the £1 million United had set aside for the deal and it then took a fortnight's wrangling before Bruce moved north.

Ferguson was planning ahead and bought Lee Sharpe, a sixteen year old who had broken into the Torquay side. United guaranteed the south-coast club a total of £180,000 in a deal based on Sharpe's progress. It was not very long before the money changed hands.

But still the manager felt that he needed to strengthen those positions where he saw flaws. In May 1988, he bought Aberdeen's Scottish international goalkeeper Jim Leighton for a record £750,000. Leighton had a remarkable record for club and country, but like his manager had to face the test of English football.

Players leaving the club were Arthur Albiston, a link with Docherty's days, and Kevin Moran who moved abroad on a free transfer.

But what about a partner for McClair? Here Ferguson played a winning hand in the eyes of United's supporters. Mark Hughes was unhappy on the continent. Barcelona realized that his partnership with Gary Lineker had not worked and had shipped him off to Bayern Munich on loan. While this was happening, United had been hit by another major blow when Gary Bailey was injured on England duty, and, like Steve Coppell before him, was

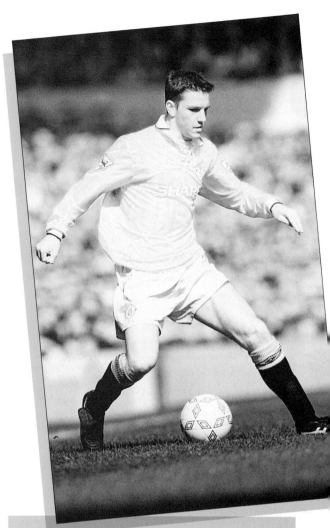

LEE SHARPE
ENGLISH INTERNATIONAL

POSITION:	Forward
BORN:	27.5.71 Halesowen, Birmingham
HEIGHT:	5ft 11in
WEIGHT:	11st 4lb
JOINED UNITED:	June 1988
PREVIOUS CLUBS:	Torquay United
UNITED DEBUT:	21 September 1988 Centenary Trophy v Newcastle United (h)

PHOTOGRAPH © ACTION IMAGES

MARK HUGHES
WELSH INTERNATIONAL

POSITION: Forward

BORN: 1.11.63 Wrexham

HEIGHT: 5ft 8in

WEIGHT: 12st 5lb

JOINED UNITED: May 1980 as apprentice
Re-signed June 1988

PREVIOUS CLUBS: Manchester United,
Barcelona, Bayern
Munich (loan)

UNITED DEBUT: 30 November 1983
League Cup
v Oxford United (a)

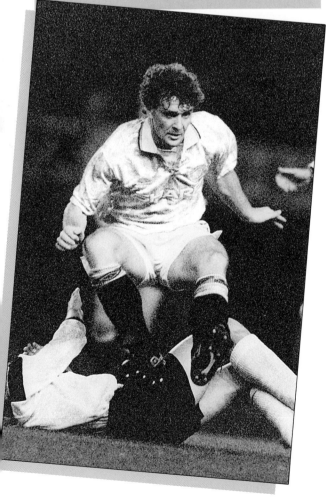

forced into premature retirement. In May 1987 Hughes came to Manchester to play in Bailey's testimonial and made it obvious that he would be happy to return to his former club if and when the time was right. He and his wife wanted to put down roots in England. The young couple had an apartment in Spain, another in Germany, and nowhere to call their home. A move back to United would give them the chance to settle down and be closer to relatives as they raised their family.

Because of tax restrictions Hughes had to stay away from Britain until April 1988, but by the time the 1988–89 season began he was a United player once again having cost Ferguson £1,600,000. Everyone waited for the goal rush, but it did not come. The Hughes–McClair strike force spluttered rather than exploded. It took five games before Hughes got onto the score sheet. He was not alone, though, because the team made a far from spectacular start, with the first goal coming after 249 minutes of football in a dull 1–0 win over Middlesbrough at Old Trafford. As for McClair, his first goal came in match six, as both he and Hughes scored in a 2–2 draw at Tottenham.

After seven League and cup games, 'keeper Leighton had conceded just one goal – a Jan Molby penalty at Anfield. But there were signs that the Scot might be finding it difficult to adjust to the English game, despite his confident start. When he dropped a harmless cross from Southampton's Graham Baker over his shoulder and into his own goal, he found himself under the microscope. In his first ten appearances he conceded just five goals, in the final ten matches of 1988 he was beaten on eleven occasions and had just three 'clean sheets'.

Ferguson's search for the right formula was constantly thwarted by injuries. He played Peter Davenport alongside Hughes with McClair on the right side of midfield and Jesper Olsen on the left. Gordon Strachan found the going tough and after being substituted in four out of seven games had doubts about his future at the club. There was unrest too for

Paul McGrath and Norman Whiteside who were openly seeking pastures new amid newspaper speculation that Ferguson was planning a clear out.

The first player to leave was Davenport, bought by Middlesbrough. A month later Jesper Olsen was sold to Bordeaux. Then Liam O'Brien began a new career with Newcastle United. Atkinson's influence was ending.

By the end of 1988 Ferguson had used twenty-four players in twenty-four games. United were fifth in the table, but losing touch with the leaders. Brian McClair had scored only half the number of goals he had hit in the previous campaign, and the support he and Hughes got from their colleagues was futile. United had been knocked out of the League Cup during a controversial game at Wimbledon's Plough Lane and a successful FA Cup run seemed the only salvation.

Then came a home win over Liverpool which not only lifted the supporters but brought a flush of excitement to the club. In only his second League game a scrawny Russell Beardsmore, barely out of his teens and built more like a jockey than a footballer, gave a performance which overshadowed his more experienced colleagues. He scored one goal and helped McClair and Hughes to find the net as United won 3–1.

Within the next ten days more youngsters were drafted in and quickly tagged 'Fergie's Fledglings' by the media.

Drawn at home to Queens Park Rangers in the Third Round of the FA Cup, Ferguson found himself forced to make changes. Lee Sharpe had 'flu and Paul McGrath was withdrawn. Mark Robins, a prolific goal scorer with the junior teams, was plunged into the side, and such was the emergency that two others, Deiniol Graham and David Wilson, found themselves on the substitutes' bench even though both had played an 'A' team game that morning.

The tie ended in a draw and by the replay four days later Sharpe had recovered and joined Beardsmore, Lee Martin and Tony Gill

Russell Beardsmore, the first of Fergie's Fledglings, who emerged in 1988 to win himself a regular place in the side until the end of the 1988–89 season. Then he slipped from the spotlight almost as quickly as he entered it when, through injury and loss of form, he found himself no longer a part of Alex Ferguson's plans. In June 1993 he joined Bournemouth on a free transfer. © *Action Images*

in the starting line-up, with Graham and Wilson on the bench. The replay went into extra time after Gill equalized, then United took the lead when Wilson crossed and Graham stabbed home, only for Rangers to force a second replay with a late goal. United won this game 3–0.

The cup run ended in Round Six when Nottingham Forest won 1–0 at Old Trafford. However, more young players were given an opportunity to make the grade as Alex Ferguson realized that United had little chance of gaining any honours. Giuliano Maiorana, a Cambridge boy with Italian parents, made his full début in a televised game against Arsenal; Robins had his League début against Derby County; and Gill delighted the home supporters with an exciting goal against Millwall just seven days after that strike at QPR.

The season ended with United in mid-table, and the Fledglings vanished from the scene as quickly as they had arrived. Deiniol Graham broke his arm badly and eventually left the club; Tony Gill ended his career when he broke his leg in March 1989; Maiorana damaged a knee so badly that he was out of action for four years; Wilson was transferred; and Beardsmore remained at the club until the championship year of 1993, but spent much of his time in the Reserves.

In March 1989 Gordon Strachan was transferred to Leeds United for £300,000, moving to the Second Division club with the words: 'My one wish is that I can return to Old Trafford in the not too distant future as Leeds celebrate promotion to the First Division and United are the champions.' Who would have thought that within the next three years and with Strachan as captain, Leeds would not only achieve their target of promotion but would beat United to the championship?

The 1988–89 season ended with unrest on the terraces. Ferguson's critics used the tabloid press as well as radio and television to snipe at the manager. Not surprisingly he hit back, refusing access to certain journalists and making it clear to former players and managers that they and their comments were neither appreciated nor welcome. Then came a period in the club's history when its activities off the field received as much publicity as those on it.

There was understandable optimism during the summer of 1989 when Ferguson spent £2 million on Neil Webb from Nottingham

Gordon Strachan claimed that he wanted a new challenge when he left United to join Leeds in 1989. He certainly got it. His career was relaunched and, after previous success with Aberdeen under Alex Ferguson, then in Ron Atkinson's 1985 FA Cup side, he collected a championship medal with Leeds in 1992. © *Action Images*

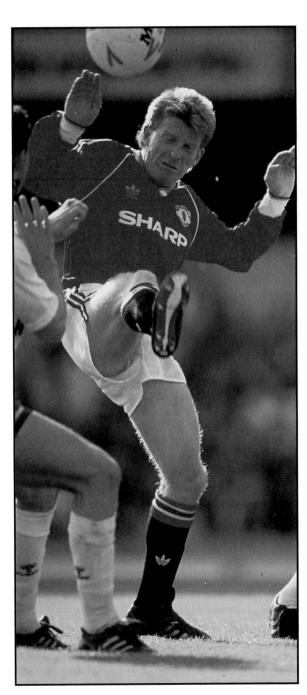

Forest and Michael Phelan, the Norwich City captain, but on the eve of the opening game of 1989–1990, it was a third party who stole the headlines. News broke that businessman Michael Knighton was about to buy into the club.

Chairman Edwards called a press conference at Old Trafford and Knighton was introduced as a man who was ready to invest cash and buy the majority shareholding. He eagerly outlined his plans, which included spending £10 million on the Stretford End: 'Clearly this is a very big day in my life. I look forward to working with Alex Ferguson, he's got my 150 per cent support at the moment.' A day later he was given a rapturous welcome as he performed a ball-juggling act in front of a 47,000 crowd gathered for the game against Arsenal. It was difficult to imagine that this was a man who claimed to be quiet and shy!

The showbiz start rubbed off on the players, who slammed the new champions 4–1 with Neil Webb scoring ten minutes from time. Mark Hughes and Brian McClair followed Steve Bruce onto the scoresheet as he put United in front after just two minutes. The manager had been criticized for his summer selling of Norman Whiteside to Everton and Paul McGrath to Aston Villa, and the head-hunters were ready to plunge, but the victory forced them into the shadows again.

With the season three games old Ferguson spent again – a record £2.3 million on Gary Pallister of Middlesbrough. In mid-September he completed the £2 million purchase of Paul Ince of West Ham, after a medical snag, and bought Danny Wallace, the speedy winger from Southampton, for £1.5 million, but only after seeing the England injury jinx strike for a third time. Neil Webb was carried off in Gothenburg after rupturing his Achilles tendon. He was ruled out for the next seven months.

By the time Webb returned to the side, Michael Knighton no longer made the headlines. The public defrocking of Knighton started when doubts were cast about his financial

GARY PALLISTER
ENGLISH INTERNATIONAL

POSITION:	Defender
BORN:	30.6.65 Ramsgate
HEIGHT:	6ft 4in
WEIGHT:	13st
JOINED UNITED:	August 1989
PREVIOUS CLUBS:	Middlesbrough, Darlington (loan)
UNITED DEBUT:	30 August 1989 v Norwich (h)

PAUL INCE
ENGLISH INTERNATIONAL

POSITION:	Midfield
BORN:	21.10.67 Ilford
HEIGHT:	5ft 11in
WEIGHT:	11st 6lb
JOINED UNITED:	September 1989
PREVIOUS CLUBS:	West Ham United
UNITED DEBUT:	16 September 1989 v Millwall (h)

PHOTOGRAPH © ACTION IMAGES

position. He had two months to come up with the capital to complete the deal, but there were many who claimed he would fail. The biggest campaign against him came from the *Daily Mirror*, the newspaper owned by Robert Maxwell whose efforts to take over United in January 1984 had themselves proved abortive.

Eddie Shah, another newspaper publisher, claimed Knighton was trying to 'sell on' the club. Martin Edwards took out a High Court injunction to stop Knighton approaching any other would-be buyer and in the United boardroom the directors were far from happy. Amer Midani and Bobby Charlton openly said that they felt that the club should be floated on the Stock Market to let the supporters take over rather than any one man.

Then on Wednesday, 12 October 1989, twelve hours before the takeover deadline, it was announced that the deal had been cancelled by mutual consent. In return for withdrawing from the purchase agreement Knighton was given a seat on the board.

That the happenings of those weeks in the autumn of 1989 turned out to be significant in the future of Manchester United, there can be no doubt. The club today is the richest in the country having been successfully floated as Manchester United plc. But if the involvement of Michael Knighton was significant in the financial development of the club, there was an event of similar importance about to occur on the field of play.

United were fifteenth in the table when the decade ended. Dreams of the championship could be forgotten for another season. Then Mark Robins scored a goal at the City Ground in Nottingham which not only won an FA Cup Third Round tie against the odds, but opened the way for United to succeed in Europe and eventually the League.

Not one round of the cup competition gave United the advantage of a home draw. They won at Hereford, Newcastle and Sheffield United without even a replay to set before the Old Trafford fans. The semi-final was a different matter and provided Manchester with a

Mark Robins, hero of United's FA Cup run, races against Denis Irwin (then of Oldham Athletic) during the 1990 semifinal at Maine Road. Later Robins would leave United to join Norwich City, while Irwin would be part of the championship side. © *Action Images*

feast. United were drawn against Oldham Athletic, the Second Division form side, which had already reached the League Cup Final. Oldham were the bookmakers' favourites to win promotion and had been using the plastic playing surface at Boundary Park to their best advantage throughout the season. Their away form was indifferent but on the synthetic grass they were a different team.

The semi-final was on a neutral ground, Maine Road, and it took two games there to settle the issue. The replay went to extra time and it was Mark Robins, the player whose goal had kept United in the competition in the Third Round, who scored the winner. The player who had lived all his life within a mile or so of Boundary Park, and whose father was a senior police officer in Oldham, destroyed his home town's dream of a first FA Cup Final. He had only been on the pitch for a few minutes, after coming on as substitute, when he got behind the Oldham defence and United won 2–1. Alex Ferguson was at Wembley.

The twists and turns of the season had seen the vultures which had been circling above Old Trafford suddenly dispersed by the scent of success. Talk behind the back of the manager was that he would cling to his job as long as United stayed in the FA Cup. Once they were out, he would be out too. The whispering came largely from the businessmen and hangers-on who would gather after games in the Grill Room, one of United's restaurants. There they would lobby the media regulars as they passed through the drinking club on their way out of Old Trafford on match days. They had their allies within the Press force, men who would seize on any opportunity to push the knife a little further into Fergie's back, while to his face wishing him good luck in the next game.

The manager's refusal to ignore damaging headlines was one reason that the anti-Ferguson brigade had emerged. He was not a man to take a beating without fighting back, especially when he felt it to be unfair. Ron Atkinson had ignored such criticism and his method of handling the media had made a 'bad

press' a rarity. Alex Ferguson was not that type of man. He seemed to prefer a 'them and us' relationship and there were numerous stories told within Press circles of confrontations between a furious manager and an apologetic journalist after he had taken exception to a particular story.

The explosions were short, sharp and swiftly forgotten, and if the United manager was a man who bore grudges he never showed it. As for the reprimanded reporters that is a different matter and in 1990 those who had been chastized thought that their moment had come. In truth it was Alex Ferguson's.

United met Crystal Palace in the FA Cup Final drawing 3–3, and almost losing to Steve Coppell's enthusiastic team. Then came a decision which revealed the true Alex Ferguson: a man who was ready to risk his future on ninety minutes of football; to take an unexpected gamble that he knew would destroy a friendship, but which would benefit his club if it came off. He put Manchester United before everything else.

During the build up to the game there had been much newspaper speculation that Ferguson was on the lookout for a new goalkeeper. Jim Leighton had played in forty-five matches including the Final, conceding goals in all but thirteen – a sharp contrast to the form he had brought down from Aberdeen. Neville Southall, the Everton 'keeper, was said to be top priority on Ferguson's spending for the approaching summer, and this threat could have had some effect on Leighton, although he denied it: 'It's never really worried me. This club is always going to be linked with players but you do not have to let it get to you. A couple of years ago it was poor Chris Turner who was having to live through all this sort of thing and it didn't worry him, and it doesn't worry me. It was the other way round for me at Aberdeen, the stories were all about me leaving to go to different clubs rather than somebody coming to take over from me.'

Leighton had other things on his mind: 'I've played in Scottish Cup Finals, won the Scottish championship, and I've got a European Cup-Winners' Cup medal. But playing in the FA Cup Final has got to be the top of them all. Hopefully winning the cup would be a great springboard for a championship campaign next season.'

Jim Leighton was right. Winning the cup did provide the key to the future . . . but he was not to be a part of it. In the weeks before the first final Leighton missed three games. He was replaced by Les Sealey, the Luton Town player who had been signed on loan by United as cover for the senior 'keeper. United had been hit by injury problems in the one true specialist department. Gary Walsh, the England Under 21 'keeper, was out of contention, Sealey stepped in.

Sealey played at Loftus Road in a League game, which United won 2–1, ending a run of ninety-two consecutive senior games for Leighton who had a thigh strain. He kept a clean sheet in the next game, a remarkable match in which United beat Aston Villa 2–0 at Old Trafford, with Mark Robins dashing the championship hopes of Graham Taylor's team with two splendid goals.

Leighton came back for the next match and United lost at Tottenham. He was rested for the following game as junior 'keeper Mark Bosnich faced Wimbledon in a 0–0 draw. With two League games left before the Cup Final, Jim Leighton returned, and he and his colleagues conceded four goals in a game at Nottingham Forest which had the critics gloating. A 1–0 win against Charlton Athletic ended Leighton's bad run, then came the final. Leighton left the Wembley pitch with his colleagues as the crowd applauded the 3–3 draw. The players were exhausted after the efforts of the afternoon and, while they were disappointed not to have won, they were also happy that the cup had not slipped away from them.

While those who had played relaxed in the dressing room an anxious Les Sealey emerged and gave the first clue of what was about to happen: 'Seen Ken Merrett [the club secretary] anywhere?' he asked. 'I've got to get re-

Alex Ferguson took the gamble of his career when he decided to leave Jim Leighton out of the side for the FA Cup replay in 1990. He won the game but lost a friend in a player who had been with him at Aberdeen before his move to Old Trafford. Leighton has since returned to Scottish football.
© *Action Images*

registered, my loan period finished today.' Sealey would be needed as cover for the replay, thought those who witnessed the short conversation. Alex Ferguson had other ideas. On the night of the replay, Thursday, 17 May 1990, when the teams were announced there was a stunned reaction from everyone – in goal for United . . . Les Sealey!

United won 1–0 – Alex Ferguson's gamble paid off. In his book *Six Years at United* (Mainstream 1993) the United manager wrote: 'If I could have my time over again I would not have dropped Jim Leighton . . . not because it

Les Sealey's dramatic inclusion in the 1990 Cup Final side was popular with United's supporters because he was a player who struck up an instant rapport with the fans as soon as he pulled on the 'keeper's shirt. He was voted on to collect a winners' medal in the League Cup final a year later and returned to the club after a spell with Aston Villa to be Peter Schmeichel's deputy during the championship season. © Action Images

(*Inset*) Lee Martin, whose winning FA Cup winning goal in 1990 had paved the way for the success, was a constant absentee over the next four years... [illegible]... scheme he appeared to have a promising career ahead... but after he broke into the side and the arrival of Denis Irwin and Paul Parker left him in the Reserves and he was transfer-listed in 1993. © Action Images

was wrong from the football point of view, but because it wrecked his career and cost him two years of his footballing life. You must remember that Jim was a goalkeeper I had nurtured as a boy. I gave him his début at Aberdeen and we had come a long way together.'

Sealey became United's first-choice 'keeper after being offered a twelve-month contract: 'I felt on the night of the game that it wouldn't be fair on any of the United players, particularly Jim, if I said anything, which is why I refused to give any interviews and you have never read a quote from me about it.

'United hadn't had the best season in the League and all I did was play in three games. I felt that after all the stick that the players had taken from the media and different people, to go on and win the FA Cup was all the talking that needed to be done. It shut up quite a lot of people.

'Jim and I have spoken about it privately and I don't think that what we said is really for public airing. What Jim feels is up to him, I know how I felt.'

No one can say whether United would have won, or lost had Jim Leighton played, but they took the cup thanks to a solitary goal from full-back Lee Martin.

Fate had had its say. Those important goals from Mark Robins had taken United to Wembley, Martin's shot won them the cup . . . Fergie's Fledglings had had their last flutter.

Celebration time for United after winning the FA Cup in 1990 thanks to a replayed final against Crystal Palace. The game gave Alex Ferguson the key to Europe and the side formed the backbone of the squad which won the championship three years later. © *Action Images*

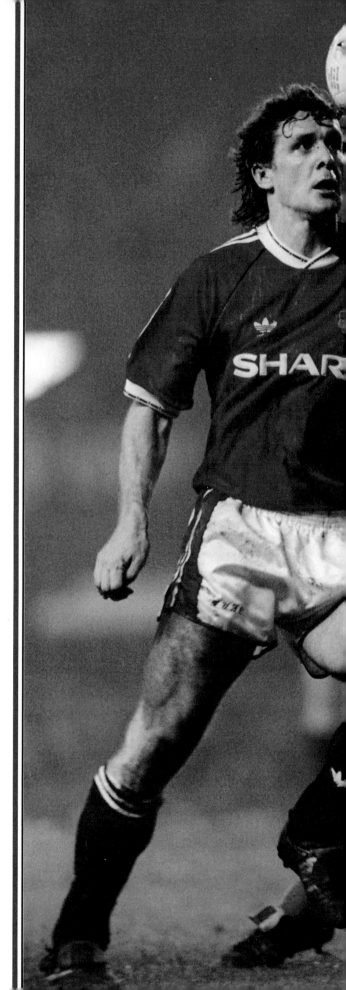

The first leg of the European Cup-Winners' Cup quarter final at Old Trafford and Mark Hughes presses forward for United as Denis Der Zakarian closes in. Zakarian missed the second game in France and his replacement, Manuel Thetis, was sent off. © *Empics/Neal Simpson*

CHAPTER FOUR

A CHAMPIONSHIP VISION

VICTORY IN THE 1990 FA CUP FINAL OPENED THE DOOR to Europe for United. For a second time the club became England's ambassadors abroad and, like Matt Busby in the Fifties, Alex Ferguson and his players found themselves under a microscope as English clubs were allowed to compete in the three European competitions once more.

Since the summer of 1985 they had been banned because of the behaviour of Liverpool supporters at the European Cup Final in 1985, when in Belgium's Heysel Stadium many Juventus fans died in an outbreak of terrace rioting which led to the collapse of a wall. During the ban United were denied European football three times, missing the Cup-Winners' Cup of 1985–86, and the UEFA competition in 1986–87 and 1988–89, but the door now reopened.

The Cup-Winners' Cup placed yet more demands on Alex Ferguson and his players and few expected them to do well on all fronts. If they were to succeed in Europe there was every possibility that their efforts in the League and the domestic competitions would suffer. This was to prove correct.

They began the new season with a 1–1 draw against champions Liverpool in the Charity Shield, and by early September had pushed into third place with one defeat in five matches. But three days before their first European fixture they lost 4–0 to Liverpool at Anfield in a game which made it abundantly clear to Alex Ferguson that there was still much to do.

After that hammering it was understandable that there was perhaps some caution in the players' steps as they faced an unknown Hungarian side, Pecsi Munkas, in front of a relatively small crowd at Old Trafford. Little-known opponents and that Liverpool scoreline had some effect on the attendance that night, as just 28,411 saw Clayton Blackmore and Neil Webb score the goals which secured an easy victory. Afterwards Alex Ferguson's comments rang true: 'I think one of the problems is that, after missing European football for five years, a lot of fans have forgotten how exciting it can be. Some of the younger ones have never seen a European game at all. You get out of the habit.'

This was Alex Ferguson's first European campaign as United manager, and having succeeded in the Cup-Winners' Cup when in charge at Aberdeen, he was determined to become the first manager to achieve that feat both north and south of the border.

The draw for Round Two was greeted with mixed feelings by the players. United were to play Wrexham, the Welsh Cup holders from less than 50 miles away, and the home town of Mark Hughes! There was optimism, though, that United would still be in the competition by the New Year. This was well founded as they won 5–0 over the two legs. For Mark Hughes there was disappointment. He missed the chance of playing at Wrexham because of a rare injury. He had dearly wanted to play at the Racecourse. However, it was to be Hughes who made the headlines in Round Three.

United met Montpellier, who had been helped in their efforts to win the French Cup, and so to qualify for Europe, by Eric Cantona, who had moved on during the summer. By the time the first leg was played at Old Trafford, interest in the competition had increased bringing in a crowd of just under 42,000.

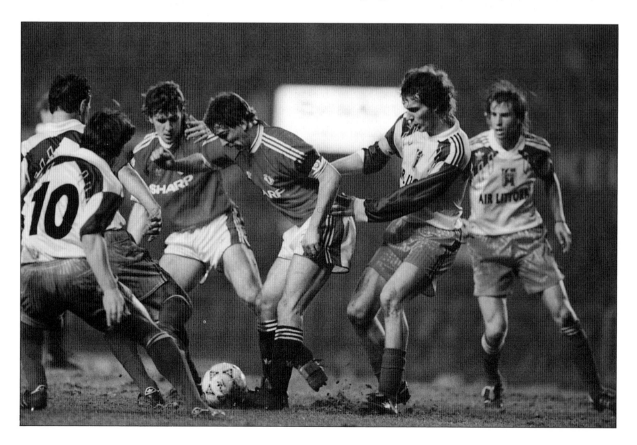

United got off to a marvellous start when within a minute McClair rifled home a Sharpe cross after Hughes had found him with a pass wide to the left wing.

Then disaster struck when the player who

Bryan Robson is hauled off the ball as he tries to keep up the constant pressure on Montpellier. Brian McClair gave United the perfect start when he scored in the first minute, but the first leg ended 1–1. In France, goals from Clayton Blackmore and Steve Bruce saw United in the semi-final. © _Empics/Neal Simpson_

United have never lost a European game in Manchester but they came close against Montpellier. After equalizing through a Lee Martin own goal the French held out for eighty-three minutes and time and again launched counter attacks. Here Lee Sharpe is outnumbered as he tries to find a way through the visitors' defence. © _Empics/Neal Simpson_

had put United in Europe scored for the opposition. Lee Martin's FA Cup-winning goal had secured the European place, but with seven minutes gone he flicked the ball past Les Sealey while trying to control it and Montpellier had the luxury of an away goal. A decisive factor perhaps.

The French were inspired and they held out against everything United could throw at them until the incident which marred the night. Mark Hughes fell to the ground after what appeared to be a head butt from Pascal Baills the full-back. Baills screamed his innocence as he was sent off. Television later proved that whilst the player deserved to be punished for violent conduct, there appeared to have been little or no contact with the United striker. 'I went down as a reaction to the attack and I stayed down until the referee sorted it out,' was the Hughes version of things.

The incident did little to cement Anglo–French relationships, nor did the Montpellier president, who made it known that Hughes would not be very welcome in France. But Hughes did stride out at Montpellier, ignoring the chants and the obscene banners written in English, and it was the Welsh who had the last laugh. Almost on half-time, Clayton Blackmore fired home a free kick from just inside the French half. Then, after the same player was brought down, Steve Bruce converted a penalty to put United in the semi-final.

By this time they had bowed out of the FA Cup with a defeat at Norwich; reached the League Cup Final, where they were due to face Sheffield Wednesday; and were holding on to fifth place in the table.

In the semi-finals they were drawn against Polish club Legia Warsaw who had beaten the favourites Sampdoria in the previous round. The first leg in Warsaw saw United fighting back after being stunned by an early goal. Within a minute McClair equalized, then Hughes and Bruce gave them a 3–1 advantage for the home leg. There was no lack of support when Legia Warsaw came to Old Trafford for the penultimate round of the tournament. Backed by the cheers of 45,000, United played cautiously taking the lead through Lee Sharpe after twenty-eight minutes before conceding an equalizer during the second half. The 1–1 draw was enough to take them to the final against Spanish giants Barcelona.

Nine days before that game, however, came

Polish 'keeper Zbigniew Robakiewicz hurls himself at the feet of Mark Hughes as United head for a 3–1 victory in the opening leg of the semi-final in Warsaw. Legia scored first but United equalized within a minute through Brian McClair, and later Mark Hughes and Steve Bruce were on target. © Empics/Phil O'Brien

(Inset) Steve Bruce puts Robakiewicz under pressure. Lee Sharpe's first-half goal gave United a 4–1 aggregate lead in the semi-final. Though the Poles equalized to draw the second leg 1–1 they could not stop the Reds reaching the Cup-Winners' Cup final for the first time. © Action Images

an event, which viewed with hindsight, could be regarded as the turning point in the club's quest for that elusive championship. Some might argue that it was little more than a coincidence, but it certainly proved that Alex Ferguson was a man of vision as well as a successful football manager.

The scene was Highbury Stadium. United had just completed one of the three remaining League fixtures of the 1990–91 season. The sound of the chanting supporters echoed around him, as Alex Ferguson walked away from Arsenal's after-match interview room. To his left, beyond closed double doors, the football ground now devoid of supporters, was littered with the debris of celebration. Streamers draped over crush barriers, pieces of torn-up paper swirled on the terracing in tiny whirlwinds of red, white and yellow confetti, while out on the pitch a group of men repaired the scars left by the game which had just ended. Other groundstaff watched as a motorized mower travelled back and forth at the far end of the stadium, its smiling driver seemingly enjoying every moment. Like his spectators he was no doubt looking forward to the celebrations which lay ahead that night.

Earlier, as the Arsenal players emerged from the tunnel they had sparked off a cascade of red and yellow balloons, which bounced on heads and hands in the crowd, before spilling over the perimeter fence. They had poured onto the pitch to explode under the feet of stewards, policemen and players, and the after-match tasks of those clearing the ground included the gathering of their tattered remains.

Behind him in the interview room Alex Ferguson left the media muttering quietly together as they compared notes. In truth, they had little interest in what the Manchester United manager had to say that night. United had played Arsenal, but the game itself was irrelevant. The result could not alter the destination of the championship trophy because it had been presented to Arsenal before the kick-off. That was the reason for those celebrations. It was Arsenal's story which would fill the back

pages of the popular newspapers the following day. Tonight was for winners, not losers.

The United manager turned towards the stairs to descend through Highbury's famous marble hall and out to the team coach. The entrance was packed with people reliving the season: the important wins; the great goals; the outstanding performances. Few noticed that United were leaving. Outside the fans were also celebrating: 'Champions, champions, champions!' Tonight was their night.

'I feel like a gatecrasher at a party, an interloper, an unwanted guest,' Ferguson said in quiet, almost embarrassed tones. He and George Graham crossed paths as the Arsenal manager went to take his turn before the gathering of the Press. Alex patted his counterpart's arm saying nothing. The managers had chatted before the game and Alex had passed on his congratulations when the two shook hands before the kick-off.

Graham was manager of the League Champions for the second time in three seasons; his pride was immense but he hid it well. Probably somewhere deep behind the calm exterior he wanted to scream and shout like those supporters outside. But he stayed silent. Once inside the interview room he took his seat on the rostrum to face a barrage of predictable questions:

'What does it feel like to be Champions again?'

'Was there ever any time during the season when you felt that it might slip away?'

'What do you plan in the immediate future?'

For Alex Ferguson his immediate future was a long journey back to Manchester where he could turn his attention to the Cup-Winners' Cup Final, but he had witnessed an event which made him look far beyond that: 'Something has happened here tonight which I feel will be of great importance to Manchester United. The players and supporters have seen what it is all about and I hope the message isn't lost. They have seen what it means to a club to be champions. To collect that trophy. I dearly hope that that it can be us having those celebrations next year.

'There is no jealousy in what I am saying. I'm not envious at what Arsenal have achieved. I don't need these nights to remind me of what winning a championship means to a club, that is quite clear to me, but perhaps the supporters do, and perhaps the players.

'Just look at the last time that Manchester United were champions and imagine what Old Trafford would be like if you took the title in the final home game of the season. That is enough to whet anyone's appetite and I think that we are quite close now.

'We can look at Arsenal, and they can look at us, and it becomes a mirror image. We have a young squad just as they do, we have a good foundation, and we have some tremendous players. We'll have a real go at it next year you mark my words!'

United ended the 1990–91 championship campaign in sixth place, seven places higher than the previous season.

	P	W	D	L	F	A	Pts
Arsenal	38	24	13	1	74	18	83
Liverpool	38	23	7	8	77	40	76
Crystal Pal.	38	20	9	9	50	41	69
Leeds Utd	38	19	7	12	64	47	64
Man. City	38	17	11	10	64	53	62
Man. United	38	16	12	10	58	45	59

In the League Cup they had pulled off a remarkable win on the Arsenal ground, inflicting not only a rare defeat on the champions-to-be, but a victory of record proportions . . . by six goals to two! The scoreline suggested that it might not be the Gunners' year after all, but it proved the exception rather than the rule, and freeing them of extra fixtures possibly helped Arsenal in the end.

That cup-tie on 28 November 1990 had provided the clubs with an escape valve to ease the pressure which followed a much publicized incident at Old Trafford a little over a month earlier. Just before half-time Arsenal had been given the lead by Anders Limpar when his shot appeared to cross the line. Television pictures later proved that referee Keith Hackett had made a mistake and that a goal should not have been given. The referee's decision may have led to the unsavoury incident in the sixty-first minute.

There was a clash involving Nigel Winterburn, the Arsenal full back, Denis Irwin and Brian McClair. Tempers flared and suddenly virtually every player was involved. Punches were thrown. The game was stopped for several minutes and the scenes filled television screens and newspaper back pages for days. The clubs were charged with bringing the game into disrepute. They were both heavily fined and had points deducted – Arsenal two, United one. Fortunately, it had little effect on the season's outcome. Had Arsenal fallen two points short of winning the title at the end of the season who knows what might have happened when the sides met on 6 May.

The days which followed those scenes at Highbury were busy ones for Ferguson and his backroom staff and Les Sealey once again found himself at the centre of things.

In the League Cup Final, United lost by a single goal to Ron Atkinson's Sheffield Wednesday. It was a dull performance by Alex Ferguson's team. During the match Sealey had badly gashed his knee. With the European final approaching he was a major doubt and there was speculation that United might have to turn to Gary Walsh, who had returned from a serious ankle operation, or the inexperienced Australian boy Mark Bosnich.

Between the two finals, Walsh became first choice playing in the second game against Legia Warsaw and the home victory over Manchester City when, on his full début, the promising Ryan Giggs took credit for the winning goal. Walsh also played in that game at Highbury, and was in goal for the game immediately before the European final, when United lost 3–0 to Crystal Palace at Selhurst Park. Here another new player was brought into the side, Ukrainian Andrei Kanchelskis.

United left for Rotterdam, where the final was staged, with Sealey still under treatment. He trained with his colleagues the night before the game and made little secret of the extent of the injury: 'It's not a certainty that I'll play because the Gaffer hasn't picked me yet. He hasn't spoken to me about the injury and I'll leave it to him. But if I'm not right in my own mind and he wants me to play then I'll tell him, because you can't jeopardize everybody's efforts through the season just for your own

(*Main picture*) Fernando Munoz – 'Nando' – the Barcelona full back will remember 15 May 1991 for a different reason than Lee Sharpe and Mark Hughes. The Spaniard was sent off as United strode through to a 2–1 win in the Cup-Winners' Cup final. Here he gets in a challenge to stop a United attack. © *Empics/Neal Simpson*

(*Above*) 'We've done it!' Brian McClair hugs Bryan Robson as the final whistle goes in Rotterdam. United have won their second ever European trophy and Lee Sharpe, Steve Bruce and Clayton Blackmore are about to join in the celebrations. © *Action Images*

(*Below*) Steve Bruce's header is going goalwards as Mark Hughes makes sure with his first goal of the Cup-Winners' Cup final in Rotterdam. The second came eight minutes later and was United's 100th goal of the 1990 – 91 season. ©*Action Images*

benefit. I know it's hard, especially for somebody like me who's spent all those years at Luton fighting against relegation and then when you get somewhere like this you're injured, but I've got to face the facts.

'It's much worse than I thought. When I did it I felt that I'd be back in ten days, but it's taken nearly a month. I've lost a lot of strength in my leg and while it's almost back to normal it's still not a hundred per cent.

'If I don't get picked I've got no complaints. The manager has got to pick what he thinks is the best team on the night, personalities don't come into it. I know it would be a shame if I missed out because I've played for the whole of the season and this is the sort of thing you aim for, win, lose or draw.

'I'd play on crutches if I have to so long as he says I'm playing. I'm not going to argue with him!'

Sealey would play, but once again Alex Ferguson had to make a decision which would have a lasting effect on one of his players. He left Neil Webb out of the starting line-up and this after the midfielder had become a regular in the side again following his Achilles injury. Webb remained at the club for another season and a half but missing the final was something the player could never forget.

Michael Phelan took his place as United lined up:

SEALEY
IRWIN BRUCE PALLISTER BLACKMORE
PHELAN INCE ROBSON SHARPE
McCLAIR HUGHES

For Alex Ferguson reaching the final was a major milestone: 'This will be a wonderful occasion for the club. The excitement in Manchester is immense – for half the population at least. It was a fairytale when Aberdeen reached the final in 1983, particularly in beating Real Madrid because we were not one of the glamour clubs. Now though it feels as if United are where we belong, playing a club like Barcelona in a European final.

'This club has had some great European nights and I know this will be another one. I realize that it is twenty-three years since United won the European Cup, but even so you feel that it is something that is meant for us.

'I remember clearly that night in 1968. I was a player with Glasgow Rangers and I watched the game on television and recall it vividly. I think that everyone in Britain was rooting for United in that game because of Sir Matt. United had a great team, there is no doubting that, but it was for the manager that everyone was hoping they could win because he had come through so much and showed what he was made of by building another team after the disaster.

'A lot of our young supporters don't realize the significance of this game, it's something unique. But there are still a lot of the older fans who were at Wembley in 1968 and this must be nostalgia for them.'

He was right. In Rotterdam the memories poured back. Law, Best and Charlton played again as Ince, Hughes and Sharpe dominated the Spaniards. Robson led his colleagues to victory and Steve Bruce sweated blood. It was 1968 all over again, but what the modest Ferguson did not realize was that the part of Busby was being played by him.

The 2–1 win came thanks to two strikes from Hughes. One as he forced home a Bruce header; the second a solo effort of spectacular proportions when he ran in from the right flank to thrust a shot into the heart of the Barcelona goal. Sealey was protected for all but one moment when Ronald Koeman scored with a free kick, but the knee held out.

Rotterdam was alive with United supporters who outshouted their Catalan counterparts and, as the media fought for after-match interviews, Martin Edwards could not hide his delight: 'It was an absolutely superb performance. Barcelona just crept back into the game towards the end, but I felt that we were by far the better side and we played in the true tradition of Manchester United. I honestly thought that this would be a very tough game and that it could go either way but we rose to the occasion.' Looking ahead the chairman added: 'Next season we'll be in five competitions, the League, the FA Cup, the League Cup, the Cup-Winners' Cup and the European Super Cup. So there is plenty to look forward to.'

Plenty? Too much perhaps.

The seed which had been sown at Highbury had germinated in little more than a week but already the hunger for better things was growing amongst player and supporter alike.

'The fans were magnificent tonight,' an elated Steve Bruce said as he and Mark Hughes watched replays of the goals on Dutch television. 'They expect big things from us and tonight we have given them something to shout about. All I want is for them to go home happy and I'm certain they will.'

For Bruce himself it was a moment to savour in a career which had taken him from Gillingham to Old Trafford via Norwich City: 'It's the first time that I have played in Europe and I'm thirty-one this year. This is a memory that will stay with me for ever . . . now all I would like to do is go a step further and perhaps win that League title.'

For Mark Hughes that game had been much more than a European final. He had been rejected by Barcelona before his return to Old Trafford and sinking the Spanish Armada had given him added delight: 'I had no axe to grind with Barcelona even though this win has given me great satisfaction. I had a chance when I was there and I didn't take it and that is history now.

'I am very much a Manchester United player and to win the cup for our fans is a great moment. There's been a few tears in the dressing room, the lads just can't believe that we've gone out and won the way we did.

'We were under a lot of pressure before this competition started because we were one of the first English teams back in Europe, and as it went on we were the only one left as the others were knocked out of the Champions' Cup and

STEVE BRUCE
ENGLISH 'B' INTERNATIONAL

POSITION:	Defender
BORN:	31.12.60 Corbridge, Nr Newcastle-upon-Tyne
HEIGHT:	6ft
WEIGHT:	12st 6lb
JOINED UNITED:	December 1987
PREVIOUS CLUBS:	Gillingham, Norwich City
UNITED DEBUT:	19 December 1987 v Portsmouth (a)

A moment to savour for Alex Ferguson as he becomes the first manager to lead an English and a Scottish club to success in a European competition. As he runs to take the cheers of the United supporters in Rotterdam he would have recalled similar scenes when he was in charge of Aberdeen when they won the 1983 Cup-Winners' Cup final. © *Empics/Neal Simpson*

the UEFA Cup, so we were carrying the flag. We knew that if we could win it then it would be a major boost for British football and perhaps that tells you how happy the lads are.'

What next?

'I wouldn't mind a championship medal.'

Alex Ferguson gripped the trophy as he added: 'This is what it is all about. Our support created an incredible atmosphere and that is Manchester United. It was the first European experience for many of the players and understandably there were some nerves in the first half, but we settled well after the break and deserved to win it. I told them that they would have to go through some pain, because you do in a European final, and they did, especially in the last few minutes as Barcelona tried to get back in the game. But it was worth it.'

The bond between manager and supporter was sealed that night as Alex Ferguson took his place behind Sir Matt Busby on Manchester United's ladder of success. To be second to Busby is no mean feat.

'They [the supporters] are magnificent. They get behind the players and urge them on and we have won this cup for them. This club is based on its wonderful support and on the traditions that Sir Matt brought here. We have just cemented that relationship. Now we have to use this success as a platform to greater things and we all know what that means.'

The rain still fell as Alex Ferguson and his players slowly drifted towards the coach which would carry them away from the Feyenoord Stadium and back to the Elysee Park Hotel for a private party. Wives and girlfriends had been flown to Holland to watch the game, and the privileged guests included United fanatic Mick Hucknall, lead singer with Simply Red.

It was a night of total contrast to their exodus from Highbury, as this time it was the shouts of the United supporters which filled the night air, 'Champions, champions'. Perhaps a little premature, unless they too had the vision of Ferguson.

Miles away in the Brainpark area of the city the media group gathered after a hectic evening. The stories were filed, the headlines written and the newspapers would be on the streets by dawn as the fans got home. Meanwhile coaches left in convoy for the ferry ports where they would haul their happy cargo back to England. A massive airlift flew thousands into Manchester, which prepared itself for the team's arrival the following night. Those who had driven over left Holland happy and England's European return had ended.

But what of Alex Ferguson's vision? Had the message of what lay ahead got to his players in the way it had obviously reached the supporters? Let Mark Hughes have the final word: 'We feel we are on the verge of something big. Manchester United will always be judged on what we do in the League and after this European success we can hopefully build on it for the championship. Who knows, next year we could be up there challenging for the title.'

Alex Ferguson went to bed at 5 a.m. after those Dutch celebrations, and a new day dawned for Manchester United.

Constant rain could not dampen the spirits of the United supporters who travelled to Rotterdam for the European Cup-Winners' Cup final in 1991. They came from far and wide including this group from Malta where the club has a big following. © *Empics/Neal Simpson*

1992 – SO NEAR . . .

WITH THE CUP-WINNERS' CUP ON DISPLAY IN THE Old Trafford museum, it was understandable that many experts were tipping United to improve their League form and finally end the years of waiting for the championship.

Winning the European trophy had released some of the pressure on Alex Ferguson and his players and there was every reason to believe that those predicting greater glory could be correct. Old Trafford had a summer of celebration as fans poured in on stadium visits and for a glimpse of the latest piece of silverware. But for the manager there was no time to rest on the laurels of success; he was thinking of the future and knew that to push for the title he had to strengthen his squad. He bought wisely, brilliantly would perhaps be a better word in the light of what was to come, and got the players he wanted.

First the giant Danish international goalkeeper Peter Schmeichel, a huge blond muscular man, who at 6 foot 4 inches certainly looked

Mark Hughes heads past John Lukic to put United through to the Fourth Round of the FA Cup in the tie at Elland Road on 15 January 1992. Having already knocked Leeds out of the Rumbelows (League) Cup a week earlier, success rebounded on United as fixture congestion hampered their championship bid and Leeds took the title. ©
Action Images

the part. He was by far the tallest 'keeper in living memory to pull on the goalkeeper's jersey at Old Trafford. Then Paul Parker, a diminutive figure compared with the giant Dane, but an England international who had shown in the World Cup during the previous summer that he had the talent to play at right full-back or centre half. Was his arrival a threat to Steve Bruce, Gary Pallister or Denis Irwin? Or were United going to use a sweeper system?

The guessing games started, but one player had no intention of waiting to discover the answer as far as his future was concerned. Les Sealey saw the threat to his career which the arrival of Schmeichel posed. He was happy to stay, but on his own terms. Ferguson offered him a one-year contract. Sealey asked for twice that.

'The manager told me that he could only give me twelve months, so when Ron Atkinson offered me a two-year deal at Aston Villa I took it,' Sealey said later. 'As it turned out, one year with United would have been better than two with Villa any time.' Sealey was to return to United as cover for Schmeichel in January 1993, after an unhappy spell at Villa Park.

The experts had to wait to see what Ferguson's intentions were when the 1991–92 season began, because a back injury meant that Gary Pallister was not fit enough to start the opening game against newly promoted Notts County. Instead, the tall defender was on the bench as Parker played alongside Bruce with Clayton Blackmore at left back and Denis Irwin right. Pallister came into the game after sixty-three minutes when Paul Ince was replaced and the reshuffle gave a hint of what was to come, with Irwin switching to left full-back, Blackmore replacing Ince in midfield, and Parker taking over from Irwin as Pallister went into his normal position.

Schmeichel and Parker were impressive, but it was two other players who captured the imagination of the 46,278 crowd. Andrei Kanchelskis had been kept under wraps since his arrival from Russia towards the end of the

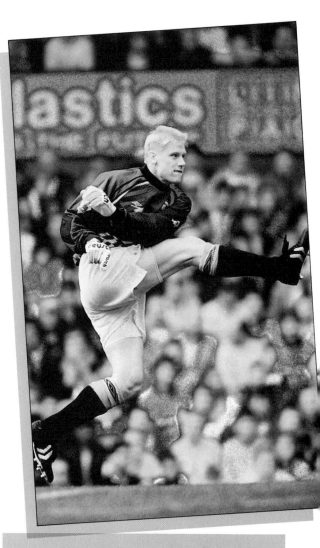

PETER SCHMEICHEL
DANISH INTERNATIONAL

POSITION:	Goalkeeper
BORN:	18.11.63 Gladsaxe, Nr Copenhagen
HEIGHT:	6ft 4in
WEIGHT:	14st
JOINED UNITED:	August 1991
PREVIOUS CLUBS:	Hvidovre, Brondby (both Denmark)
UNITED DEBUT:	17 August 1991 v Notts County (h)

PAUL PARKER
ENGLISH INTERNATIONAL

POSITION:	Defender
BORN:	4.4.64 West Ham, London
HEIGHT:	5ft 7in
WEIGHT:	10st 9lbs
JOINED UNITED:	August 1991
PREVIOUS CLUBS:	Fulham, Queens Park Rangers
UNITED DEBUT:	17 August 1991 v Notts County (h)

PHOTOGRAPH © EMPICS/NEAL SIMPSON

previous season. The young Ukrainian spoke no English so the club hired the services of George Scanlan, a former language professor, to interpret. Kanchelskis spoke with his feet and the Old Trafford fans understood every word. He was extremely fast, an orthodox right winger who seemed capable of reading situations quickly and getting into useful positions. His style of play perhaps needed some adjustment but the promise was there for all to see.

The second of the duo came into the action in the seventy-sixth minute after Hughes and Robson had scored the goals which would secure three points. Ryan Giggs, the boy who, like Kanchelskis, had tasted first-team football the previous season, brought a tingle to the spine when he touched the ball. Giggs was a product of the scouting system which Ferguson had set up soon after his move south. Brian Kidd and Nobby Stiles had worked together to set up Schools of Excellence, which held coaching sessions for boys of all ages. Tiny tots to teenagers played football under the umbrella of Manchester United and the talent coming through was impressive. That Alex Ferguson appointed Brian Kidd as his assistant, when Archie Knox left to take up a similar post with Glasgow Rangers, is all that needs to be said of the way the manager viewed the role of the former United star.

Young Giggs had played for England Schoolboys on his way to the top level but he was known then as Ryan Wilson. His parents had moved to the Manchester area from their home in Cardiff when his father, Danny, signed for Salford Rugby League Club. Ryan was a toddler and had lived in Salford since that time. However, following his parents' divorce Ryan opted for his mother's name, becoming Ryan Giggs and declaring his nationality as Welsh. How England must rue that day!

The slim, dark-haired teenager played only a quarter of an hour against Notts County, but his speed and skill showed through. Alex Ferguson was determined that Giggs would not be rushed into the senior side and threw a protective arm around the boy, banning the media from speaking to him and gradually introducing him into the team. Giggs was an unused substitute for the second game of the season which was against Ron Atkinson's new club Aston Villa.

The former United manager had enjoyed his days at Sheffield Wednesday, his victory over Ferguson's team in the 1991 League Cup final proving particularly satisfying and he had topped the season by winning promotion through the Second Division play-off system. But he found the offer of the manager's job at Aston Villa something he could not refuse, even though for a while he tried to.

Atkinson's first game in charge of Villa was away to Sheffield Wednesday, his second at home to Manchester United. Such is the finger of fate. Villa won at Wednesday, but another good display by Schmeichel and a Steve Bruce penalty gave United a second victory. Schmeichel's presence had added confidence to United's make-up and, after four games without conceding a goal, the back pages were predicting that the long wait for the title might finally end in 1992.

The opposition had to score at some time, and it was Lee Chapman who proved that Schmeichel was not invincible, when Leeds came to Old Trafford for the season's fifth game. The Yorkshire club took the lead early in the first half and it was five minutes before the end when Bryan Robson equalized to keep his side at the top of the table and still unbeaten.

But it was the style of football United were playing which had everyone talking. They were not just winning games, they were entertaining, something which had always been demanded by the Old Trafford faithful. The fans might even forgive a defeat if the football was exciting, but a boring, tactical, 1–0 victory meant nothing.

This was a United team like those long gone, solid at the back, exciting in attack, and there were many who saw in the teenage Giggs a ghost from the past. Slim, golden-skinned,

ANDREI KANCHELSKIS
RUSSIAN (NOW UKRAINIAN) INTERNATIONAL

POSITION:	Forward
BORN:	23.1.69 Kirovograd, Ukraine
HEIGHT:	5ft 10in
WEIGHT:	12st 4lb
JOINED UNITED:	August 1991
PREVIOUS CLUBS:	Dynamo Kiev, Shaktyor Donetsk (both Ukraine)
UNITED DEBUT:	17 August 1991 v Notts County (h)

RYAN GIGGS
WELSH INTERNATIONAL

POSITION:	Forward
BORN:	29.11.73 Cardiff
HEIGHT:	5ft 11in
WEIGHT:	9st 8lb
JOINED UNITED:	July 1990 as apprentice
PREVIOUS CLUBS:	None
UNITED DEBUT:	2 March 1991 v Everton (h)

PHOTOGRAPH © EMPICS/NEAL SIMPSON

fast, brave and with wonderful control, he reminded many older supporters of George Best, and when he scored the final goal of a 3–0 win over Norwich City the memories came

flooding back. Giggs had the ball at his feet as he attacked Bryan Gunn's goal. He took on the big Norwich goalkeeper leaving him stranded before cutting towards the bye-line. It looked for a moment as though the ball might roll out of play but Giggs knew what he was doing. Spinning on his right foot he hammered in a shot which ripped into the roof of the net. It seemed an impossible angle from which to score and it was that which made the goal all the more spectacular . . . that and the memory of Best doing exactly the same thing against Sunderland in 1969!

Making comparisons between Giggs and Best brought the wrath of Alex Ferguson, as well as the supporters, on those who dared. 'Football Pink' editions of the *Manchester Evening News* regularly ran letters for and against the subject, but only those who regularly saw Best play as a teenager and now looked at Giggs knew the truth.

Pat Crerand perhaps knew Best better than any of those who now looked at Giggs: 'I played with George for many years and I know exactly what people are talking about when they link him with Ryan. There are parts of his game which remind you of George. It isn't just folk hoping for a return to the past and nobody is saying that Ryan is another George Best. He is a Ryan Giggs. Two different players playing at two different times but you cannot hide the fact that he reminds you of somebody else.'

A 1–0 victory over Southampton at The Dell kept United top of the table. Leeds were making their presence felt with an unbeaten run comparable with United's, but the Reds were opening up a gap.

By the end of September, with ten games played, Leeds were in second place, but Alex Ferguson's pace-setters were firm title favourites:

	P	W	D	L	F	A	Pts
Man United	10	8	2	0	18	3	26
Leeds Utd	10	5	5	0	16	6	20

As well as making a challenge for the title, United had also to defend the Cup-Winners' Cup and they soon began to realize that new rules brought in by UEFA would seriously handicap them. Scots, Welsh and Irish players were classed as 'foreign' in the eyes of official-dom and their numbers restricted. It meant that when United met Greek club Athinaikos as their defence began, Giggs, Blackmore, Kanchelskis and Donaghy were not allowed to play. With Parker injured and Robson suspended following a booking from the previous campaign, two of the Fledglings had to be called into the side. Mark Robins and Russell Beardsmore started the game, with Reserve team players Neil Whitworth, Paul Wratten and Paul Sixsmith on the substitutes' bench alongside Danny Wallace, who was unable to command regular selection, and replacement goalkeeper Gary Walsh.

A struggle against the obviously inferior Greek side was followed by defeat in Spain by Atletico Madrid, who found flaws in the Schmeichel make-up with a 3–0 victory. United were out of Europe by the time they had completed fifteen League games, and they were also off the top of the table. A home draw against Liverpool gave them their first point of October as Leeds lost ground by going down to Crystal Palace at Selhurst Park. That was their first defeat and two games later came United's. In between, champions Arsenal came to Old Trafford with memories of that controversial game a season earlier, which cost both clubs points and money. This time there was no flare up as Arsenal took the lead through David Rocastle and Steve Bruce equalized. It was another home draw, the third of the season.

With Denis Irwin now the established left full-back, even though he was a naturally right-footed player who occupied the right-back position for the Republic of Ireland, Paul Parker returned after missing nine games through injury. In his absence Mike Phelan had played right back, but had been plagued by a knee ligament problem since pre-season and was sidelined for the trip to Sheffield

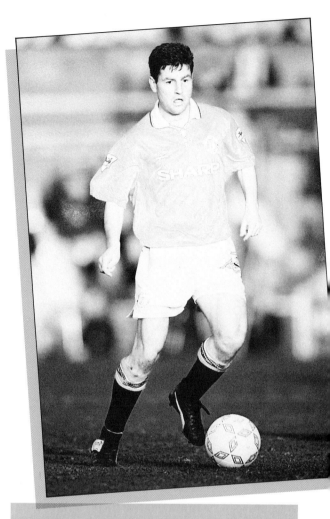

D E N I S   I R W I N
REPUBLIC OF IRELAND INTERNATIONAL

POSITION:	Defender
BORN:	31.10.65 Cork, Republic of Ireland
HEIGHT:	5ft 7in
WEIGHT:	9st 7lb
JOINED UNITED:	June 1990
PREVIOUS CLUBS:	Leeds United, Oldham Athletic
UNITED DEBUT:	18 August 1990 Charity Shield v Liverpool (Wembley)

PHOTOGRAPH © ACTION IMAGES

Wednesday. Mark Hughes was suspended after being sent off during the game against Liverpool when he and Gary Ablett, who was also dismissed, were involved in a wrestling match. Mark Robins was also banned after being sent off in a Reserve game, and with Paul Ince out through injury the strength of the squad was tested to the limit. United started the game:

SCHMEICHEL
PARKER BRUCE PALLISTER IRWIN
KANCHELSKIS WEBB ROBSON GIGGS
BLACKMORE McCLAIR

Wednesday went ahead through Hirst after fourteen minutes, but McClair hit back with two goals in the next eight minutes. The first after he intercepted a Warhurst back pass, the second a close-range shot when the home side failed to clear the ball. United led until the seventieth minute when Nigel Jemson, who had come on as substitute three minutes earlier, scored the first of two goals which won the game for Wednesday, his second coming in the last ten minutes. It was the thirteenth game of the campaign and it proved unlucky for United.

Rivals Leeds made up for their defeat with three successive wins, while United drew with Manchester City at Maine Road before beating West Ham at Old Trafford, when Giggs got his third of the season, and Crystal Palace 3–1 in London.

United had collected the European Super Cup as their first trophy of the season beating Red Star Belgrade at Old Trafford in a game which had lost its attraction because of the civil war in Yugoslavia. Normally, the fixture would have been played over two legs but it was impossible to travel to Belgrade, so UEFA opted for one game and a lone goal from Brian McClair secured victory.

United were also involved in the League Cup, beating Cambridge in the two-legged second round. Teenage goalkeeper Ian Wilkinson had been thrust into the side for the second leg when Gary Walsh cried off through

illness and Schmeichel was away on international duty. Wilkinson played in front of a hostile crowd at the Abbey Stadium as United defended a 3–0 advantage and was beaten only two minutes from time when Dion Dublin blasted home a fierce shot for Cambridge to make it 1–1 in the second leg.

Portsmouth were beaten 3–1 in Round Three, and United began December with a 2–0 victory over Oldham to reach the quarter-final stages of a competition the club had yet to win. Then fate took a hand and it was perhaps this moment which decided the destiny, not of the two domestic cups, but of the League championship.

Immediately after that victory over Oldham, the draw was made for the next round . . . Leeds versus Manchester United at Elland Road. Three days later the draw for the Third Round of the FA Cup threw up an identical fixture. It was an incredible irony. Not only were the top two due to end 1991 with their return League fixture in Leeds, they would now clash three times in seventeen days.

'I can't believe it,' said Alex Ferguson when he heard the FA Cup draw. 'I know we are both going well but this is the sort of clash you expect in a semi-final or some late stage of the competition.

'Mind you I'd rather have this sort of game than the giant killing ties you sometimes get. So I'm happy enough with the draw and not the slightest bit worried about it. The great thing is, it's a big game and this club can handle big games. You know that somewhere along the line in a cup competition you're going to face this kind of hurdle; now it's up to us to get over it.'

The League battle continued and December brought the kind of form which convinced even the most cynical of the critics that United were in with a good chance of ending the twenty-five-year drought. They beat Coventry 4–0 at Old Trafford as Leeds won 2–0 at Luton. Then it was a 3–1 Sunday victory at Chelsea on 15 December which took them back to the top, because Leeds had drawn 1–1 at home to Tottenham on the previous afternoon. Neck

Another European trophy for United as they beat Red Star Belgrade in the Super Cup final in November 1991. It was a final tinged with sadness as civil war in Yugoslavia saw the virtual break up of the famous club. Here Andrei Kanchelskis makes it East against East as he takes on left back Goran Vasilijevic. © *Empics/Steve Etherington*

(*Inset*) The big Englishman versus the big Irishman. Gary Pallister uses every centimetre of his 6ft 4in frame to out-leap the equally tall Niall Quinn of Manchester City during the 1991 Maine Road derby. © *Action Images*

and neck into Christmas and then came an amazing game at Oldham.

'It was a throwback to the good old days,' Alex Ferguson proclaimed after United had beaten Oldham 6–3 at Boundary Park in a Boxing Day fixture which was packed with incident. 'Once upon a time you would get scorelines like 7–2 and 5–0 on Boxing Day for one reason or another and this was one of those games. It was entertaining, it was cavalier and it must have been great for the fans.

'I think the thing is we are always looking like scoring nowadays. We have so much penetration in the side that you expect goals.'

Little did the manager know at that point in time that it would be a lack of such attributes which would make a major contribution to the outcome of the season.

By the turn of the year the top of the table was:

	P	W	D	L	F	A	Pts
Man. United	20	14	5	1	41	7	47
Leeds Utd	22	12	9	1	38	17	46

A point clear, two games in hand. Surely this was it.

The first of the three clashes with Leeds saw United without Bryan Robson, who had strained a calf muscle during the Oldham game. Denis Irwin was another absentee. It was a blow for him because Leeds was the club which had rejected him as a youngster. He had moved to Oldham and established himself as a top-class player. Irwin had scored twice against his old club in the Boxing Day romp, but he missed a chance to show that Leeds were wrong to let him slip through their net.

Lee Sharpe was back though. The youngster, who had been sidelined all season following a hernia operation, was named as one of the substitutes and played in the dying minutes of a game which, according to Reds' goal scorer Neil Webb, United deserved to win: 'We knew that Leeds would come at us during the first quarter of an hour and they did, but we survived that onslaught and we got a great start in the second half with the goal. But when you are away from home you should really hold on to things like that. They got a fortunate penalty decision, I don't know whether the referee was right or not, and that was that.

'This was a good result though, mark my words. To take a point at Elland Road is something. The atmosphere was amazing, Leeds are flying and we knew it would be hard. It's going to stay that way till the end. They haven't lost at home and neither have we and it's going to be a battle.'

Three days later United had lost at home. The new year began badly, very badly for United. They faced Queens Park Rangers at Old Trafford and tried to hide the fact that several players were suffering from the effects of 'flu. They were hammered 4–1 with Dennis Bailey scoring a hat-trick and Andy Sinton adding the fourth. It was humiliating and rumours spread that the reason for the defeat was that the players had been drinking into the early hours of the morning as they let in the new year. This was totally untrue. Not only had there been no alcohol consumed the previous night, but Alex Ferguson had kept his squad together in a local hotel and all of them had been in bed long before the celebrations began.

The rumours were typical of those spread by anti-United scandalmongers, as was the one which swept the Elland Road Press room before the next game with Leeds – the reason Ryan Giggs had not been interviewed by radio and television was because he had a speech impediment. This equally untrue allegation was actually believed by some journalists because it had apparently appeared in a Leeds Fanzine! Such is life with Manchester United.

Leeds had gone back to the top by winning 3–1 at West Ham as United lost at home. A week after the QPR humiliation came the second of the three meetings. This time there was a winner. United ran away with the game, beating Leeds 3–1 in front of their stunned supporters whose hopes were built up when

Gary Speed opened the scoring. United hit back. Clayton Blackmore hammered in a fierce free kick, then Kanchelskis shot from close range after being set up by Giggs, and finally, the teenager himself scored as he threw himself feet first at a low cross from Parker. The show was back on the road.

A Kanchelskis goal brought victory over Everton at Old Trafford and this was followed by a 1–1 draw at Notts County. Then United took over the top spot once more on 22 January after beating Atkinson's Villa 1–0 thanks to a Mark Hughes goal.

Perhaps at the time it was difficult to spot, but Alex Ferguson knew that something was going wrong. The side which was scoring goals for the fun of it during the run up to Christmas was now having problems. Between 23 November and Boxing Day, United scored eighteen times in five League matches. From 29 December to 22 January, the total was just five, one per game.

A visit to Highbury produced the third consecutive away draw and four days later came the disappointment of becoming the first Division One club to be knocked out of the FA Cup on the new penalty shoot-out rule. This was introduced not to streamline the competition, but because of demands made by the police authorities. They claimed that they needed a clear ten days between rearranged games in order to organize policing, so the Football Association decided to end replays from the penalty spot if scores were still level after extra time.

The third visit to Elland Road had again resulted in victory for United, leaving them in both the cup competitions, while Leeds had only the championship to occupy their thoughts. The FA Cup tie was one Leeds felt they should have won, for they dominated for much of the night until Mark Hughes scored as he headed down a Giggs cross. So United were in the Fourth Round and a 0–0 draw at The Dell brought Southampton to Old Trafford. United never led during the game, but staged a late fightback to level at 2–2 in the last minute of normal time. The extra half hour failed to produce another goal and in the end Southampton won the penalty competition 4–2.

There were sixteen League games remaining, and a home draw with Sheffield Wednesday was enough to give United the top spot again. Leeds, who had been unbeaten since the start of October, lost their second game. Amazingly, it was at Oldham, the scene of United's big victory, and Joe Royle's team did Alex Ferguson a favour coming out 2–0 winners. The time was now right for United to accelerate away from Leeds.

Mark Hughes scored both goals in a 2–0 win over Crystal Palace, but draws against Chelsea and Coventry made it a slim margin between first and second after thirty games.

	P	W	D	L	F	A	Pts
Man. United	30	17	11	2	51	22	62
Leeds Utd	30	16	12	2	55	24	60

United's involvement in the League Cup was a double-edged sword. They beat Middlesbrough over two legs to reach a Wembley final against Nottingham Forest, but the fixtures were piling up as the end of the season approached. This and the lack of goals was to be their downfall.

Leeds had been given free rein by their failure in those two cup matches and had strengthened their squad in sensational style by signing Frenchman Eric Cantona, who it was thought had been about to join Sheffield Wednesday. He was an unknown quantity, but after Lee Chapman was injured in the FA Cup tie, Howard Wilkinson was forced to make a move. Chapman returned after missing four games with a broken wrist. He and Cantona were on the scoresheet for the 2–0 win at home to Luton, which closed the gap on United to one point.

March came with Leeds ahead in the race but they had played three games more than United and their form was slipping. They drew at

home to Aston Villa, won at Tottenham and then, like United, felt the strength of QPR, losing 4–1 at Loftus Road. But then they rallied, beating Wimbledon 5–1 at Elland Road with Chapman hitting a hat-trick and Cantona again involved, and followed this with two draws, one at Highbury and the other at home to West Ham.

As for United, they beat Sheffield United at Bramall Lane and lost away to Nottingham Forest before a home draw with Wimbledon and the visit to QPR. Lambs to the slaughter? Not really. It ended 0–0 and United remained second with two games in hand.

Alex Ferguson took his players to Norwich knowing that they had the ability to win the championship, provided the fixture congestion did not get too much. But he could see problems ahead. A 3–1 win at Carrow Road eased matters and there to watch the game was Prime Minister John Major who said afterwards: 'This is the first time that I have actually seen Paul Ince play in a live game and I must say that I was very impressed.' It was hardly a surprise, because Paul scored twice as the Prime Minister looked on, and gave an outstanding display as Brian McClair added the third. But was the Prime Minister watching the champions elect? 'From what I have seen today they have every chance of taking the title.'

Perhaps he was being diplomatic but there was a ring of truth in Mr Major's words because United were now top with a game to spare. The championship race looked as if it would take an important turn during the following week when Manchester City were due to play both of the leading clubs in the space of three days: Leeds on Saturday, 4 April and

(*Previous page*) **After the disappointment of losing to Sheffield Wednesday in 1991, United returned to Wembley the following season to win the League Cup for the first time. Here Darren Wassall challenges Mark Hughes and Steve Bruce as Roy Keane (then a Forest player) helps out.** © *Empics/Neal Simpson*

then United as they prepared for the League Cup final at Wembley. City beat Leeds 4–0 at Maine Road and the headlines proclaimed, 'Thanks neighbour' as Blues' supporters told United fans that they had done the job for them. If United could now beat City in the Old Trafford derby, the gap would open . . . they drew 1–1!

Five days later, and for a moment thoughts of the championship were pushed into the background as Steve Bruce led United out at Wembley. There had been plenty of speculation that Bryan Robson might return, after being out since part way through the game at Norwich with a calf strain, but the club captain made his intentions clear in the build up to the final: 'We are going for the championship and that is what I want more than anything else. If I can get fit for Wembley then I will play, but I won't take any chances. I would rather miss the final and be fit for the next game against Southampton than miss the League match.'

Another player also missed the Wembley showpiece, but not by choice. Just as he had done a year earlier when United beat Barcelona in the Cup-Winners' Cup, Alex Ferguson named a line up which did not include Neil Webb. Instead, he opted for Michael Phelan as he had in Rotterdam, even though Webb had been a regular for most of the season.

After reaching the final for the third time in the history of the competition, United won the League Cup. Alex Ferguson had achieved something that even Sir Matt had not and he looked on proudly as his players paraded the trophy after a Brian McClair goal beat Brian Clough's Nottingham Forest.

United returned to Manchester, but there was hardly time to enjoy the cup win before the next game, four days after the final, as the fixture congestion began to tell. United were being forced to play five vital games in the space of eleven days, starting with that Southampton fixture which, like the final, Bryan Robson missed. United won 1–0 as Andrei Kanchelskis avenged the penalty shoot-out.

Two days later the injuries began to take hold. Paul Parker limped off at Luton and would take no further part in the season because of a hamstring strain. There were still no Paul Ince or Bryan Robson as United hung on to draw 1–1. Mark Hughes was carrying an injury and played just eighty minutes both at Luton and in the next game.

Just forty-eight hours after Luton, United were at home to Nottingham Forest and Brian Clough's side stunned Old Trafford by winning 2–1, pushing United down to second place. But Leeds had played a game more – there was still a chance.

	P	W	D	L	F	A	Pts
Leeds Utd	40	20	16	4	70	35	76
Man. United	39	20	15	4	60	29	75

Two days after the Forest disappointment, United met West Ham at Upton Park. On paper it was a game they seemed certain to win. West Ham had already been relegated and were by far the inferior side. Many United supporters had circled this game on their fixture list as the championship battle progressed, knowing how fitting it would be if the twenty-five-year wait ended where it had started. It was at Upton Park in 1967 that United had sealed their last championship. Could they do the same in 1992? In 1967 United won 6–1, but 1–0 would do this time.

It was not to be. United's luck ran out in the sixty-sixth minute of a game they had dominated. Mark Hughes almost scored with a spectacular bicycle kick and West Ham chased downfield as the ball was hacked out of their goal. Gary Pallister intended to kick the ball back towards his forwards but it struck the advancing Ken Brown who was striding towards Schmeichel's goal. No-one was more surprised than the West Ham player when the ball shot from his leg and into the back of the United net.

Alex Ferguson refused to admit that the race was over but it was easy to read into his words what he must have been thinking after the 1–0

defeat: 'It's been a terrible night for us, one of those nights that just knocks you flat. They played it like a cup tie and West Ham fought really hard. It makes you wonder where they would be in the League if they had been fighting as hard as that all season, but there's a few teams who have been doing that to us recently.

'I felt that Forest on Monday tried harder than they did in the Cup final, and I know their supporters won't like what I say but it's a fact. But while we've been up against this sort of thing, from our own point of view we haven't scored enough goals since the turn of the year and that has been a worry for us.

'Tonight we had young players up front who perhaps lacked the experience to finish teams off . . . but next year they'll be better. We aren't giving in but for the first time I've got to say that we are now in such a position that we are praying that Sheffield United beat Leeds on Sunday. Leeds only have to win two games to win the championship and we can do nothing about it.'

Alex Ferguson was left to ponder on what to do next and was fully aware that things had gone sadly wrong for United after the turn of the year. Before that defeat by QPR, United had scored forty-two times, but between New Year's Day and the West Ham game they had managed only eighteen goals.

And so came Sunday 26 April 1992, a day which will be remembered for all the wrong reasons by United followers. The fixture list had caught up with itself thanks to the glut United had fought through, and the leaders each had two games remaining: Leeds away to Sheffield United and at home to Norwich; United away to Liverpool and ending the season with a home clash against Tottenham Hotspur.

Leeds won at Bramall Lane in a game which, at times, reached comical proportions. Defensive errors let Rod Wallace score and Sheffield's Brian Gayle put through his own net as the game finished 3–2. Because the kick-off times were staggered, United's game at Anfield kicked off after the final whistle in

Ray Houghton chases Ryan Giggs during the League game at Anfield on the day the championship slipped beyond United's reach. Liverpool won 2–0 and Leeds were crowned champions after earlier beating Sheffield United. A year later Houghton was a member of the Aston Villa side which was runner-up to United. © *Empics/Neal Simpson*

Yorkshire and in the executive lounge the Liverpool fans watched in glee as Leeds celebrated. The message was clear when United ran out at Anfield: they knew that only victory would keep them in the chase. Even then they would have to rely on Norwich beating Leeds at Elland Road while they beat Spurs, for the championship to be theirs.

Anfield was a cauldron of hate as United ran out. The feelings of Liverpool supporters towards Alex Ferguson and his players were obvious as United were subjected to a barrage of derision from the first whistle. The moment had come and United were not good enough. Bryan Robson and Paul Ince had both declared themselves fit, even though this was not so, but this was an afternoon for men not boys and they fought like tigers to try to salvage the season.

Ian Rush, who throughout his career had been unable to score against United, did so in the twelfth minute. It was a low, calculated shot from the Welshman, beyond the grasp of Schmeichel who dived in vain. United piled back looking for salvation and Liverpool held out as time and again chances came and went. Then with three minutes remaining it was all over. A scramble in the six-yard box and a far-post tap-in by Mark Walters after the ball had rebounded from the upright. Leeds were champions.

The home supporters celebrated as if it was their side which had succeeded, and the players walked slowly off the pitch, United downcast, Liverpool offering the hand of consolation at the end of a long journey. They slowly trudged to the dressing room and behind a closed door kept their grief to themselves. But they were distraught. To be so near . . .

No-one was hiding, especially not Alex Ferguson who had seen the signs ahead of everyone else: 'This is just something that we will have to get over, and at this moment in time there is no point in analysing Manchester United. It's a time when, on behalf of everyone at Old Trafford, I have to congratulate Howard Wilkinson on a marvellous achievement.

'Winning the championship is an achievement. It's a terribly hard League and people who have said that it has been mediocre this season are talking absolute nonsense. This is the League clubs have been winning every year since football began. What happpened this season is that United and Leeds got off to a flyer, stayed the course right to the end, and clubs who made mistakes suffered. United and Leeds carried the banner the whole way, and it is unfair for anyone to say Leeds have won a mediocre League.'

But Ferguson realized also that there was something to be gained from the experience his players had gone through, which would perhaps count in their favour for the next campaign: 'Manchester United took their character onto the field and showed what they can do. Ince and Robson refused to come off even though they were in pain, the players didn't leave their character in the dressing room.

'They're upset of course, but a disappointment like today can be tempered by what it gives the young ones and the older players who have never really experienced real defeat in the way that it has happened to us this week. Perhaps it will make them better men and hopefully next season we will be able to go for it again. We are young enough, and good enough, and maybe we will get the breaks next time.

'This though has been a good season. We have lost the League but it has still been a good season. We have entertained. We have produced some good football at times, and we came close.

'Mark my words, we'll go for it next season!'

Brian McClair's fifteenth-minute goal gave United a 1−0 win over Nottingham Forest in the 1992 Rumbelows (League) Cup final. Eight days later Forest got their revenge. Their 2−1 win at Old Trafford virtually ended United's hopes of winning the championship. © *Action Images*

'We Are the Champions,' they sang, time and time again. Old Trafford was a chanting, smiling, flag-waving sea of happiness as old and young joined in the celebrations. They sang before the game, during the win over Blackburn, and were still singing long after the lap of honour had ended and it was time to go home. © *Action Images*

Whoever left them, he or she was without doubt a Stretford Ender who wanted to be close to that place at that time.

The newspapers that morning had acclaimed the new champions and there were pictures of Steve Bruce and Mark Hughes standing together toasting their success, and of Alex Ferguson in golfing attire smiling broadly.

He had not watched the Villa–Oldham game on television. 'I went for a game of golf with my son Mark and we were walking down the seventeenth fairway when I said to him that Villa must have won the game because if they hadn't somebody would have come out of the clubhouse and told us.

'I played up to the green and was just standing over the ball about to putt when I heard a car door slam shut. I looked up and saw this stranger running towards me over a little hillock on the course shouting, "You've won the championship, you've won the championship." I don't know who he was, but I have never been so delighted to meet anybody in all my life.'

Whether Alex was playing Mr Cool by avoiding the televised game or was too nervous to watch is his secret, but without doubt he handled the run in to the title superbly. Time and again he was asked at after-match interviews if it was getting to him, and each time his reply was the same: 'There is nothing I can do now. Just sit back and watch my players. I have done all I can do, now it's up to them.'

While Old Trafford was being prepared for the game against Blackburn, the manager spent the morning relaxing in bed. His job was complete for the time being at least, but it was the dawn of a new era. 'Now we have finally ended the years of waiting we can look ahead. Winning the title will take an immense amount of pressure off the players who have had to carry that burden for so long. Now we will see what they are really made of, and I am looking forward to next season and the challenge of Europe.'

By mid-morning there were thousands around the ground even though tickets had been sold out for weeks. United had been forced to restrict sales to regular supporters and those who had joined their membership scheme. This was an idea brought to the club by Bobby Charlton, who saw in a similar operation at Barcelona that here was a way of making supporters feel part of the club as well as generating capital. Over 60,000 became part of Manchester United as the scheme reached a peak, and in 1992–93 when numbers were kept down because of the rebuilding work, there were 50,000 members. Not all could, or wanted to, come to games, but those who did were given priority for matches such as tonight's.

How many of those gathering, as the workers took their lunch break, had tickets for the game was impossible to say. Many were fans from outside the area who had come to the stadium before looking for a place to park the car and then eat lunch. Others were buying souvenirs – flags, scarves, anything with the word 'champion' on it, which they would hoist that evening – from the club Superstore – a far cry from the days of Frank Gidley's souvenir shed which stood outside the Stretford End.

Some were on the lookout for tickets. Others were selling them. The touts were demanding vast sums from those willing to pay. 'Anything from £150 to £250 for a game like this,' one revealed as he and his colleagues weighed up the field. 'The punters are going mad for them. Ronnie sold most of his last night as soon as he got down here and they were fighting to get them. Foreign geezers most of them – Swedes, Danes and that sort. Plenty of cash in their pockets because their money goes further over here. They think nothing of paying over the odds.'

He had plenty of tickets for sale but refused to say where they had come from. 'They're genuine though,' he was quick to point out, aware that the club and the police had issued a warning for supporters to be on the lookout for forgeries.

'I must have cut the same bit of grass about twenty times, the neighbours thought I was barmy. Up and down the lawn I went and it's only eight yards square, then Frank from across the road came out of his house with a bottle of champagne in his hand and two glasses. I realized what had happened, took the grass box off the mower, tipped the lot over my head and kicked the box over the garden wall, nearly broke my toe. God it's all over, we're champions, champions.'

There were tears in his eyes and he turned to hide them by staring up at the office block which bridges the huge entry tunnel between the stadium's main reception and the ground itself. 'I bet he'll sup some champagne this week, and good luck to him.'

He was United chairman Martin Edwards, whose office overlooks the area where supporters were starting to gather even though the game was more than eleven hours away.

The BBC local radio's outside-broadcast car was parked on the road beyond the large frontage to Old Trafford on what was once Warwick Road, but which during 1993 was fittingly renamed by the local council to become Sir Matt Busby Way. The early arrivals were interviewed: assistant secretary Ken Ramsden; supporters who had made an early morning pilgrimage; some who looked as if they were still going home from the celebrations which had hit Manchester the previous night; anyone willing to talk about their feelings on that memorable morning.

A photographer wanted to take a picture of a cleaning lady polishing the trophy and had been told to wait. The championship trophy had been delivered two days earlier, housed in a large wooden box and carried into safe keeping by Ken Ramsden and 'Ned' Kelly, the man responsible for ground security. The superstitious hoped it was not a premature gesture by the Football Association and that things would not go wrong for United at such a late stage. There was no need to worry.

The photographer was allowed in once his request had been cleared and his task was completed. Twelve hours earlier he would have got an even better picture as vast numbers gathered outside the ground for no reason other than to say that they had been there on the night United won the title. Television cameras recorded the moment as they cheered and drank their way through hundreds of cans of beer.

Then Lee Sharpe turned up: 'I just wanted to see what was going on. I heard there were plenty of fans outside the ground and I wanted to be with them.' He deserved a bravery award for such a risk because as soon as he was recognized the supporters surrounded him in an affectionate mob, lifted him off his feet and carried him shoulder high in a procession around the forecourt as they yelled, 'We are the champions!'

In the bright morning sun the debris left by the revellers was being cleared away, even though there would be more to follow later. At the opposite end of the ground, down beyond the tall wooden fence erected by the builders transforming the Stretford End from terraced shrine to luxury grandstand, stood four empty champagne bottles. They were partly hidden by a huge steel gate which had been pinned back to allow the television workers access and had been left there, like milk bottles on a doorstep, as another reminder of the night before.

Champagne at the Stretford End? Why not? There are many who mourn the loss of that section of the ground where for decades the driving force behind the Old Trafford support watched its football. In the Sixties this was the place to be. Even though it has been altered beyond all recognition, for the old Stretford Ender it still echoes with memories. Could it be that whoever left those empty bottles had been someone who had stood in the crushing mass behind Harry Gregg's goal? Or perhaps it was Alex Stepney he saw, stalking the goalmouth like a caged tiger as down at the other end of the pitch Denis Law scored and he felt his breath being momentarily taken away as those behind pressed forward for a better view.

DAWN OF A NEW ERA

I T IS 8 A.M. ON MONDAY, 3 MAY 1993. IT IS A BRIGHT morning, blue skies over Old Trafford, a crispness in the air as the sun has yet to take effect. So early in the day it would be fair to expect the stadium to be deserted but already it is alive with activity as teams of workmen haul huge pieces of equipment from a fleet of vehicles parked on the forecourt outside the ticket office. They carry their burdens around the perimeter of the pitch where it becomes clear that these are the advertising boards, which during tonight's game will magically switch from sponsor to sponsor, attracting the eyes of millions watching on television.

At the Stretford End crews are running cables into the stadium for the broadcast itself, while on the pitch the United groundstaff begins the final manicure. Others are arriving for work, greeting their friends not with the usual 'Good morning,' but today with a huge smile, even an embrace and at the least a warm shake of the hand. Today is different: last night Manchester United became champions!

'Did you see it? Did you watch the match? I couldn't bear it. Listened to the commentary on Piccadilly. Kept switching off when I knew that Oldham were winning, then back on again and they were still in the lead.'

'I went in the garden and the wife shouted out, "They've scored." I thought, "Oh, sod it, but if we beat Blackburn what does it matter." I thought she meant Vanilla were winning.'

They painted the town red . . . and when that was finished they painted themselves! The fans were gathering outside Old Trafford from early morning as the longer wait ended. Eleven hours is nothing compared with twenty-six years and this trio cannot remember the last time United were champions. © *Empics/Rui Vieira*

How tickets fall into the hands of touts has been the subject of great debate for many years. Once it was a way for players to make an extra bonus, but not today. In a world of superstar wages at the big clubs, would a player risk his reputation to make a tax-free £50 when he earns £5,000 a week? Hardly.

Two policemen were approaching, so the tout scurried away, possibly unaware that he and his colleagues had been under constant surveillance since their arrival. Old Trafford is scanned by television cameras which beam pictures back to police headquarters at nearby Chester House or into the control room within the stadium.

Beyond camera range at the Salford End of Sir Matt Busby Way a white van pulled up. The driver got out, leaving the engine running, and his passenger stepped quickly round to open the rear doors. Three men walked towards the vehicle and were each handed a bundle. They split these into manageable numbers, draped the bulk over one arm then, holding out a sample, set about their business: 'Souvenir T-shirts, Premier League champions' T-shirts. Five pounds for your T-shirt.' They were attracting customers before the van pulled away and had been doing so since the previous night when they did the same in the pubs of Manchester.

On the opposite side of the road another entrepreneur was taking a step towards his first million by selling championship flags made of alternate squares, two red, two green. 'Manchester United – first Premier League Champions.' The legend was printed in white on the red squares alongside an outline of what was meant to be the new trophy.

'Championship banners . . . championship banners . . . who wants a championship banner?'

More money changed hands and soon the forecourt was awash with supporters wearing the unofficial T-shirts and sporting flags. It was more like a carnival than the build-up to a football match.

'We've come from Donegal. Got in this morning and came straight here. He's been crying most of the way, the big "idjut", now look at him.' The 'idjut' was a six-foot, dark-haired Irishman with blue staring eyes which showed clearly that he had been weeping. Like a small child he had those tell-tale streaks on his cheeks where the grime of the journey had been washed off by his tears. He wore the yellow-and-green jersey United had issued to commemorate their 100th year of League football and he was drunk. Still six hours before kick-off and he was drunk.

'They were tears of joy,' he said as he swayed in the sun. 'It's over. It's over.'

More police were being drafted in as it became obvious that the Bank Holiday game was going to attract thousands without tickets. They ignored the drunken Irishman, hoping no doubt that he would sober up before any action was needed and began checking that those around them had tickets. Anyone without a ticket was quietly advised that they should clear the area before very long, and by 3 p.m. the police operation was in full swing.

It had to be because the area between the Stretford End and the forecourt was jammed full of spectators waiting for the players to arrive. They were expected within the next hour and the commissionaires on the main door were worried that they might not be able to cope with the masses pressing towards the entrance in a deafening sea of people, chanting what else but, 'Champions, champions.'

'They've gone mad, absolutely bonkers' said George on the main door. 'Have you ever seen anything like this?'

Mounted police took over, walking their horses slowly under the tunnel and coaxing the crowd back out towards the daylight at the forecourt end. Crush barriers were placed across the area and the fans kept beyond them as the noise built up.

Inside the stadium, with four hours to go before the kick-off, Martin Edwards was preparing himself for a meeting of the Plc board. He had been interviewed by television and now stood in the main grandstand with Sir

Roland Smith, chair of the public company, before they would both go into the boardroom to hear that half-year profits of £5.5 million had been achieved, and thanks to the championship shares were at a record high.

Martin Edwards wore a huge grin, and it was not because of the financial situation: 'Well it's been a long wait and when you wait for something for twenty-six years it gives you every reason to smile.

'I've been chairman for thirteen years and before that my father held the position. He won two championships in his time as well as the FA Cup and European Cup, and although the club has been reasonably successful on the cup front in my time, the League was always the thing that I wanted and I know that is what the supporters wanted too.

'Now we have a full set of domestic honours. We have won the League, the FA Cup and the League Cup under Alex Ferguson and that is something to be proud of.

'As far as the club's financial position is concerned, we are very healthy and it proves that the flotation worked, and as the money was used to develop the Stretford End, and that work is being completed on time and within budget, that gives me something else of which to be proud.'

Looking to the future he added: 'There are tremendous prospects ahead for us when you look at the achievements of the Youth Team for example. They won the FA Youth Cup last year and reached the final again this time and I think that there are some very exciting times ahead.

'I think that Alex Ferguson has done a tremendous job. A few years ago when one or two supporters were calling for his head, we knew that he needed time. You only have to look at the work he has done behind the scenes at this club to see what great things he has achieved. It's not always about the first team. Fans tend to judge a club on what the senior side does, but there is more to it than that, and Alex Ferguson has been responsible for our strength.'

When Martin Edwards succeeded his late father he had two main aims and both were being achieved at the same time: 'I wanted the championship, and I also wanted to see Old Trafford completed. This summer the building work will be finished and the championship trophy will be in the cabinet.

'Now we are also in Europe in the European Cup, the real one. It was very nice in Rotterdam a couple of years ago, and nobody can take that away from us, but the real big one is the Champions' Cup and you only have to think back to 1968 to know what it means to this club. It would be marvellous if we could have a really good go at that next season.'

He turned to go to his meeting as Sir Roland Smith added simply: 'If you don't enjoy tonight you are not a United supporter.' He was right, it was easy to identify those who followed United, even if they were policemen, photographers or commentators who were on duty. Each wore a broad smile.

Outside the cheering got louder; the players were arriving, each running the gauntlet from the car park to the sanctuary of the Grill Room restaurant and using many different routes to get through the supporters.

'There's so many of them, you put your life at risk,' gasped a breathless Gary Pallister. 'And what about Sharpie last night. I couldn't believe it, fancy coming down here, it's a wonder he's still alive. He is isn't he?'

Lee was there, along with the rest, ready for their pre-match meal, happily signing autographs and accepting the congratulations of the restaurant staff, security men, and anyone who could get close enough. Handshake after handshake, pats on the back, hugs and smiles all round.

Understandably, there were high spirits in the camp as Alex Ferguson relaxed the rule that players either wear smart suits or their club blazers on match days. Three of them had decided to try to outdo one another when it came to the choice of jacket. Ryan Giggs, Paul Ince and Paul Parker were the centre of attraction. Giggs in a design which looked like a

(*Right*) Oh, yes! Ryan Giggs runs towards his colleagues after watching his free kick bend beyond the reach of Bobby Mimms. Blackburn's lead has been rubbed out and United are on their way towards a 3–1 win as the fans celebrate. © *Action Images*

(*Below*) A quarter of an hour into the second half and Paul Ince slips the ball beyond Bobby Mimms to put United 2–1 up. It was a game Alex Ferguson wanted to win even though the title race was over. 'I didn't want us to end the campaign with seven defeats during the season, six was enough and the players knew that. They did themselves and the club proud.' © *Action Images*

(*Right*) He has a black eye – a souvenir from a first-half clash with a Blackburn player – he is exhausted after a tension-packed season but Gary Pallister has plenty to smile about. He has just scored his first Premier League goal and United's third of the night. All three scorers celebrate, Ryan Giggs got the first and Paul Ince the second, Andrei Kanchelskis runs over to join them. © *Empics/Neal Simpson*

Something for forwards to fear in another decade as six-year-old Kaspar Schmeichel joins his dad as the celebrations start at Old Trafford. With twenty-two 'clean sheets' in all games during the 1992–93 season Schmeichel senior played a vital role in the title win. Will Kaspar one day follow in Dad's footsteps? Well he certainly looks the part. © *Action Images*

French onion seller's jersey but with narrower hoops, Ince in a gaudy black and white check, and Parker, taking the prize for taste, in a navy and white striped number with matching waistcoat.

They were ribbed from the start of their snack until the end, their colleagues covering their eyes as if dazzled by the collection, and Brian McClair summed things up when he asked Ryan Giggs if he could adjust the vertical hold on his jacket!

Alex Ferguson warmly accepted the congratulations which came his way and smiled his way through to his office where he could ponder for a while. He had already answered one question. Throughout the season Steve Bruce had been captain of the side in the absence of Bryan Robson, but now that Robson was back, even though he was only substitute tonight, the manager had decided that both players should go up to collect the trophy.

For Robson it meant the end of a long journey. He had at last been part of a championship-winning side, starting just four games, but coming on as substitute in nine others.

'It's brilliant. People have been talking about it taking twenty-six years for Manchester United to win the title, but I remember about seventeen years ago being top when I was at West Brom just after Christmas, and then being overtaken by Liverpool who went on to win the title while we finished fourth.

'I have wanted the title since then and finally I've got it, so it gives me a great deal of personal satisfaction, but as far as United are concerned we came so close last year and we knew what it was like to lose it. People were saying that last year's experience helped us, but as far as I'm concerned the one main factor is that we were out of the League Cup early and that is a competition which gets in the way of the championship and it gives you a backlog of fixtures. This year we had a clear run and the players were fresh in every game we played and proved that they were the best team in the country.'

Bryan was right. United's early exit from the two cups helped their League campaign, and even those missed penalties in Moscow seemed acceptable now. He was quick to point out that the season had not finished, that even though the race was won there were still two games to play and tonight was Blackburn Rovers: 'Yes, it's going to be a carnival atmosphere and everybody's going to enjoy that, but we are just hoping that we can put in a really good last home performance for the fans and show them that we would have won it without anyone's help, because they deserve it as much as the players.'

As for going up for the cup with Steve Bruce: 'It's going to be a special moment and while we know that the result doesn't mean anything in terms of the League Championship now, we want to finish on a high and we are going to try to get a good result.'

Then it would be back to the celebrations which Steve Bruce revealed had started at his

B R Y A N   R O B S O N
ENGLISH INTERNATIONAL

POSITION:	Midfield
BORN:	11.1.57 Chester-le-Street
HEIGHT:	5ft 11in
WEIGHT:	11st 12lb
JOINED UNITED:	October 1981
PREVIOUS CLUBS:	West Bromwich Albion
UNITED DEBUT:	10 October 1981 v Manchester City (a)

home the previous evening. He had invited 'a couple of the lads' over to watch the Villa game and once it had finished the entire team was there. 'There were three or four of us to start with and I think that the lads must have been sending smoke signals because before I knew it every one of them was there. We had a couple of glasses and a few more glasses and we had a nice time. All the players and their wives just sat and talked about what had happened. So this morning I had the job of clearing up after them and I was left to wash all the dishes!'

After the washing-up the man who had led Manchester United in thirty-seven Premier League matches had sat quietly reading the newspapers where the story of United's success was paramount. 'The headlines said we were champions and I thought to myself that was just why I had come to United in the first place. I've spent five and a half years at this club so far and I've loved every moment of it. When they signed me, I said at the time that I couldn't believe that Manchester wanted me. But when I look back on the last twenty-four hours and I realize what it means to people, I am glad that I have been a part of it.'

The Blackburn players had arrived and were in the dressing room close to where Steve was standing as he added: 'All I want now is for us to win tonight and that would make it a perfect ending to a perfect day.'

The gates had opened and the supporters were taking their places when the Blackburn players walked from the dressing room area and down the players' tunnel to the pitch. What they witnessed there brought a comment from Kevin Moran. The former United star, now skipper for Kenny Dalglish's side, told one of the crowd stewards: 'It's a bit like being the uninvited guest at a party.'

Remember what Alex Ferguson had said at Highbury that night in 1991 when George Graham's club took the title? The United manager had also said, 'Imagine what the scenes at Old Trafford would be if we paraded the

(*Above*) Even though a cordon of stewards, police and other staff encircled the Old Trafford pitch, a handful of supporters broke through to embrace their heroes as the championship trophy was paraded. However, a similar celebration planned for Selhurst Park six days later had to be abandoned because of the threat of a pitch invasion. © *Action Images*

(*Right*) Le Roi de Old Trafford! There are many who claim that Eric Cantona has taken over where Denis Law left off in the Sixties. Then the fans would chant 'Denis Law – King,' and there can be no doubting that today's supporters feel the same way about the Frenchman who played such an influential role in the championship campaign. Before Cantona arrived, United had scored just eighteen goals in seventeen League games, after his move from Leeds they netted forty-nine in twenty-five matches. © *Action Images*

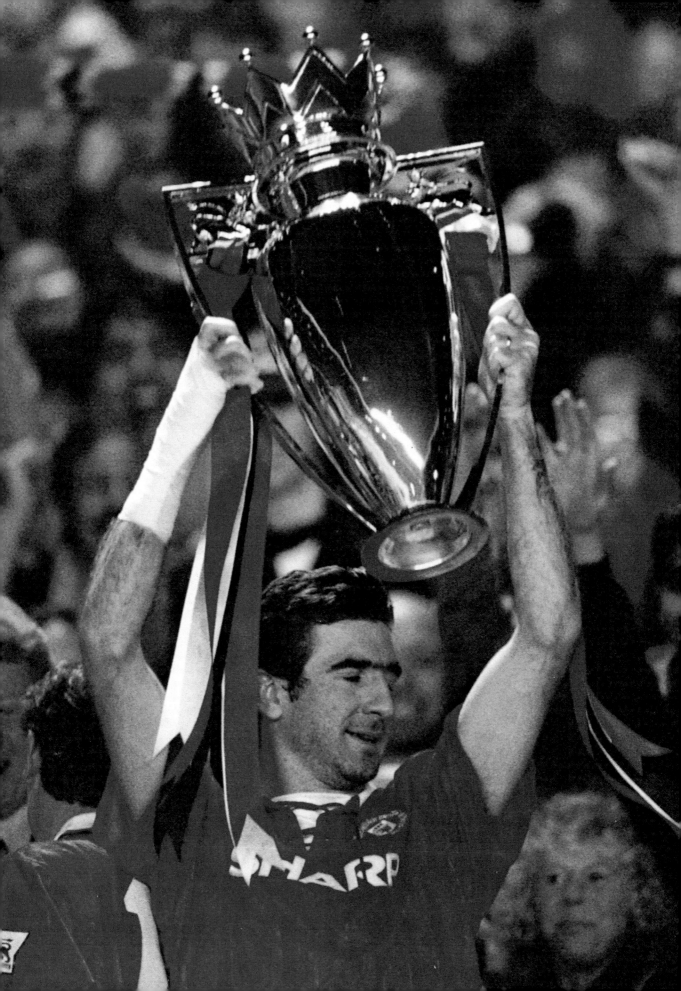

championship trophy.' Now it needed no imagination, it would happen within the next three hours.

It is difficult to find words which can satisfactorily describe the scenes within the stadium. As the loudspeaker system blared out the Queen hit, 'We are the Champions', the crowd saw it as their signal to rise in their seats, hands holding scarves and banners above their heads while they swayed and sang. United supporters had adopted the Monty Python's 'Always Look on the Bright Side of Life', as another of their theme songs and time and again this was broadcast for them to join in.

There were the balloons, the banners and the streamers. The old United cup final records from 1983 and 1985 filled the air. 'Glory Glory Man United', they sang in a never-ending din of sheer enjoyment, for it was a night of glory.

They cheered George Best, Pat Crerand, Denis Law and Bill Foulkes as they made their way from the main stand to the Sky Television studio, built high in an unfinished section of the Stretford End, where they would be interviewed. They applauded as the trophy was carried along the running track and up to the same studio for its appearance before being returned to the presentation rostrum.

In the Director's Box Joe Glanville, who for many years had been the mainstay of the vibrant supporters' branch on the island of Malta, wiped a tear from his eye as 'We are the Champions' started again. Around him the seats were filling as kick-off time approached and the roar which greeted the teams when at last they came out following their pre-match warm up some half an hour earlier surpassed everything that had yet been heard that night. The champions were on the field. Time to sing it again.

The match itself, while not irrelevant, seemed of little consequence for the first half hour. The singing went on even though Blackburn took the lead through Kevin Gallacher after just nine minutes. Oh tough, United were going to lose, what did it matter?

The players had other ideas. After twenty-two minutes, United were awarded a free kick outside the Blackburn penalty area at the Scoreboard End. The spot from where the kick was to be taken was more or less in line with the right-hand post as Ryan Giggs looked towards Bobby Mimms's goal. He stepped forward and hit a shot of such precision that Mimms had no chance, he grabbed fresh air as the ball passed beyond his reach.

It was the signal for Old Trafford to erupt. Giggs was swamped by his colleagues, it was a goal so fitting for the occasion. On the back row of the Press Box Wilf McGuinness punched the air as he leapt to his feet, turning back towards the executive club seating and roaring at the top of a voice that is far from minute. Six seats away Pat Crerand was applauding as on Piccadilly Gold Tommy Docherty said: 'What a goal, I can't believe it. Perhaps the goalkeeper should take a bit of the blame for that one because he was nowhere near it, but would any goalkeeper have saved it?' Those men of the past were watching the player of the future and at half time the crowd rose as one to applaud the players off the field.

In the dressing room it was Alex Ferguson's time to get his message across. 'We've got to win this game. We can't afford to lose it for one reason . . . and I'll tell you what that reason is, we don't want to be winning the championship with seven defeats behind us. We've lost six games this season and that's enough, we don't want to make it seven.' There was passion in his voice and the players understood as they wiped away the sweat and took on liquid to replace the toil of the first forty-five minutes.

Outside they still sang and a giant flag was passed along the whole length of the North Stand, ferried on a sea of hands, making the curious wonder how the owner gets what must be a huge bundle to a game, and how their property is recovered again at the end of its journey.

The second half was about to start.

Before the game Alex Ferguson had threatened that at half time he would withdraw any player who had not given his all during the first forty-five minutes. Whether Lee Sharpe fell into this category or not was for him to decide, but Sharpe took Bryan Robson's seat on the bench. The crowd saw the substitution and roared its approval. 'One Bryan Robson, there's only one Bryan Robson,' they sang, and his wry smile acknowledged the cheers.

An hour of the game had gone when Eric Cantona combined with Paul Ince to create the second goal. Twice the Frenchman fed the ball to Ince who hit a shot on the run and the ball ballooned the Stretford End net.

The night air was filled with the sound of 40,447 voices as United supporters screamed their delight and Blackburn followers groaned as Rovers slipped behind. There was no way back. Now came a display of superb football and the team which had tilted the championship in Alex Ferguson's direction by beating Aston Villa 3–0 on the day United beat Crystal Palace at Selhurst Park bowed to the champions.

There were more moments to savour. A 'Mexican wave' which had the Blackburn fans joining in, rapturous applause for Kevin Moran as he left the field when Dalglish made a substitution, and a juggling act from Ryan Giggs, which was proof once again that there is some of George Best in him.

'I thought for a moment it was George Best running down the wing,' wrote David Meek of the *Manchester Evening News*. 'Young Ryan Giggs was bouncing the ball on his foot as he sped towards goal and I could have sworn it was the Irish imp in action again.

'Alex Ferguson's young team has a lot in common with the team which last won the championship under Sir Matt Busby. There are talented stars like Giggs woven into great teamwork in the way of the side which triumphed in the League twenty-six years ago.

'That flash of almost nonchalant ball control from the teenaged Giggs summed up for me that United at last have a team capable of the sustained success enjoyed for so long by Sir Matt.' Meek, who has covered United since his predecessor was killed in the Munich Air

ERIC CANTONA
FRENCH INTERNATIONAL

POSITION:	Forward
BORN:	24.5.66 Paris
HEIGHT:	6ft 2in
WEIGHT:	13st 7lb
JOINED UNITED:	November 1992
PREVIOUS CLUBS:	Auxerre, Bordeaux, Montpellier, Nimes, Leeds United
UNITED DEBUT:	6 December 1992 v Manchester City (h)

PHOTOGRAPH © ACTION IMAGES

Alex Ferguson and his assistant Brian Kidd hoist the Premier League trophy before the lap of honour ends the season at Old Trafford. The partnership came together following the departure of Archie Knox to Glasgow Rangers and there can be no doubting its success. Under the duo, United won the European Cup-Winners' Cup, the European Super Cup, the Rumbelows (League) Cup, then the Premier League championship and have won more League games over the past two seasons than any other club. © *Action Images*

(*Inset*) The lap of honour is well underway as the cheers of thousands ring out at Old Trafford. The stadium has never seen anything like it as the years of waiting have ended and United are champions at last! © *Empics/Rui Vieira*

Disaster, was looking to the future like so many that night.

The game itself was yet to finish and Gary Pallister who needed half-time attention after a knock in the eye will cherish the last moments for ever. United were awarded a free kick a yard outside the Blackburn penalty area. Pallister became the twelfth player to score a League goal during the championship campaign. The fierce shot ignored the Blackburn wall as the ball buried itself beyond Mimms. The whistle went and the game was won.

A handful of supporters ignored the many pleas and broke through a cordon of police, stewards and gatemen, which surrounded the pitch, but the rest of the crowd stayed in their places, standing as some applauded, some cheered and some wept with joy as together Bryan Robson and Steve Bruce climbed the steps to collect the huge trophy.

The cup was passed one by one to those who had played their part during the season. Player after player then hoisted the trophy above their heads as the crowd cheered. They formed a team group for the army of photographers kept in a taped-off area at the side of the pitch and bobbed up and down singing 'The Bright Side of Life' as the cameras clicked. They smiled and waved, and finding that the crown-shaped lid of the cup could be worn, passed it from head to head.

The lap of honour began, a stroll of ecstasy for every player, from Ryan Giggs who has supported United for as long as he can remember, to Andrei Kanchelskis whose roots lay far away beyond what they once called the Iron Curtain. The fans shouted until they could shout no more, and after the players had left the pitch to be faced with a barrage of microphones and television cameras, the crowds poured away from the Theatre of Dreams where tonight a dream had come true.

Watching it all from his seat in the Directors' Box was Sir Matt Busby who then made his way to the dressing room below. There he said his thanks and passed on his congratulations to the boys who had carried on where his players left off twenty-six years earlier and to Alex Ferguson the man whose vision had made it possible.

Now that the ghost had finally been laid, what does the future hold for the champions of '93? Can they retain their trophy as did the Babes in 1956 and 1957? Or will there be a two-year wait before the title returns as there was between 1965 and 1967? Or could it be the year 2019 before Old Trafford sings 'We are the Champions' again?

Surely not. But although no-one knows the answer, the signs are there that the success will continue. This is the dawn of a new era for Alex Ferguson's Manchester United – Champions . . . at last!

Despite the efforts of Steve Bruce, Sheffield United's Alan Cork wins the ball as the Reds fail to pick up a point in their opening Premier League game at Bramall Lane. © *Empics/Neal Simpson*

STATISTICS

PREMIER LEAGUE 1992–93

		P	W	D	L	F	A	Pts
1	Man. United	42	24	12	6	67	31	84
2	Aston Villa	42	21	11	10	57	40	74
3	Norwich City	42	21	9	12	61	65	72
2	Blackburn	42	20	11	11	68	46	71
5	QPR	42	17	12	13	63	55	63
6	Liverpool	42	16	11	15	62	55	59
7	Sheff. Wed.	42	15	14	13	55	51	59
8	Tottenham H.	42	16	11	15	60	66	59
9	Man. City	42	15	12	15	56	51	57
10	Arsenal	42	15	11	16	40	38	56
11	Chelsea	42	14	14	14	51	54	56
12	Wimbledon	42	14	12	16	56	55	54
13	Everton	42	15	8	19	53	55	53
14	Sheff. Utd	42	14	10	18	54	53	52
15	Coventry	42	13	13	16	52	57	52
16	Ipswich	42	12	16	14	50	55	52
17	Leeds Utd	42	12	15	15	57	62	51
18	Southampton	42	13	11	18	54	61	50
19	Oldham Ath.	42	13	10	19	63	74	49
20	Crystal Pal.	42	11	16	15	48	61	49
21	Middlesbro'	42	11	11	20	54	75	44
22	Nottm Forest	42	10	10	22	41	62	40

MATCH DETAILS 1992–93

Sheffield United (1) 2 Deane (5, 50 pen)	**Manchester United (0) 1** Hughes (71)
SHEFFIELD UNITED: Tracey, Gage, Barnes, Gannon, Beesley, McLeary, Bradshaw, Lake, Cork, Deane, Hodges. Subs: Bryson (for Hodges), Kelly, Hartfield (for Gannon).	MANCHESTER UNITED: Schmeichel, Irwin, Blackmore, Bruce, Ferguson, Pallister, Kanchelskis, Ince, McClair, Hughes, Giggs. Subs: Phelan (for Ince), Dublin (for Kanchelskis).

United were up against it from the start when Paul Ince was injured in a clash with Blades' goalkeeper Simon Tracey. Shortly after this, Brian Deane scored the new Premier League's first goal. Mark Hughes put the Reds back in with a chance but a Deane penalty five minutes into the second half took the points.

P	W	D	L	F	A	Pts	Psn
1	0	0	1	1	2	0	–

Manchester United (0) 0	**Everton (1) 3** Beardsley (44), Warzycha (80), Johnston (89)
MANCHESTER UNITED: Schmeichel, Irwin, Blackmore, Bruce, Ferguson, Pallister, Kanchelskis, Ince, McClair, Hughes, Giggs. Subs: Dublin (for Giggs), Walsh, Phelan (for Ince).	EVERTON: Southall, Harper, Hinchcliffe, Ebbrell, Watson, Ablett, Warzycha, Beardsley, Rideout, Horne, Ward. Subs: Beagrie (for Rideout), Kearton, Johnston (for Warzycha).

Everton played like potential champions, tearing United apart. The critics had a field day claiming the Reds had not recovered from the disappointment of losing the championship race to Leeds. On this display few could argue.

P	W	D	L	F	A	Pts	Psn
2	0	0	2	1	5	0	22

22 August   **OLD TRAFFORD**   **31,704**

Manchester United (0) 1
Irwin (57)

MANCHESTER UNITED:
Schmeichel, Irwin, Blackmore, Bruce, Ferguson, Pallister, Kanchelskis, Phelan, McClair, Hughes, Giggs.
Subs: Dublin (for Kanchelskis), Walsh, Webb (for Blackmore).

Ipswich Town (0) 1
Kiwomya (56)

IPSWICH TOWN:
Forrest, Whelan, Thompson, Stockwell, Wark, Linighan, Williams, Goddard, Johnson, Dozzell, Kiwomya.
Subs: Youds (for Dozzell), Baker, Milton (for Whelan).

The first point of the season, but it was a battle all the way. Chris Kiwomya gave newly promoted Ipswich the lead after 56 minutes. Sixty seconds later Denis Irwin hit a tremendous shot, running onto a cross from the right and the climb up the table began.

P	W	D	L	F	A	Pts	Psn
3	0	1	2	2	6	1	20

24 August   **THE DELL**   **15,626**

Southampton (0) 0

SOUTHAMPTON:
Flowers, Kenna, Adams, Hurlock, Monkou, Moore, Speedie, Cockerill, Dixon, Dowie, Benali.
Subs: Lee (for Dowie), Hall, Andrews.

Manchester United (0) 1
Dublin (89)

MANCHESTER UNITED:
Schmeichel, Phelan, Irwin, Bruce, Ferguson, Pallister, Dublin, Ince, McClair, Hughes, Giggs.
Subs: Kanchelskis, Walsh, Wallace.

Summer-signing Dion Dublin scored his first goal to give United victory, but they left it late. A Darren Ferguson free kick was helped on by Brian McClair and as Gary Pallister headed down Dublin was on the spot to ram the ball home before the whistle.

P	W	D	L	F	A	Pts	Psn
4	1	1	2	3	6	4	11

The balance and skill of Ryan Giggs is seen clearly as he shields the ball despite pressure from Paul Goddard of Ipswich. Giggs stole the headlines throughout the season leading to hotly denied speculation that he was the £15 million target of AC Milan. The PFA Young Player of the Year was also voted Barclay's Young Eagle of 1993. © *Action Images*

Glory for Dion Dublin as he scores his first goal for United. It turned out to be his only success during the championship chase. The unlucky striker broke his leg two games after winning the points with this late shot at Southampton. © *Empics/Phil O'Brien*

Nottingham Forest (0) 0

Manchester United (1) 2
Hughes (16)
Giggs (50)

NOTTINGHAM FOREST:
Crossley, Laws, Pearce, Wilson, Chettle, Keane, Crosby, Gemmill, Clough, Bannister, Woan.
Subs: Orlygsson, Marriott, Black.

MANCHESTER UNITED:
Schmeichel, Phelan, Irwin, Bruce, Ferguson, Pallister, Dublin, Ince, McClair, Hughes, Giggs.
Subs: Blackmore (for Phelan), Walsh, Kanchelskis (for Hughes).

Three more points away from home and the campaign started in earnest. Paul Ince's effort led to the first goal when he had a shot blocked, but from the rebound Mark Hughes blasted low from 20 yards.

Goal number two came when Clayton Blackmore crossed from the right for Ryan Giggs to head home.

P	W	D	L	F	A	Pts	Psn
5	2	1	2	5	6	7	8

Manchester United (0) 1
Hughes (89)

Crystal Palace (0) 0

MANCHESTER UNITED:
Schmeichel, Blackmore, Irwin, Bruce, Ferguson, Pallister, Dublin, Ince, McClair, Hughes, Giggs.
Subs: Kanchelskis (for Dublin), Walsh, Martin.

CRYSTAL PALACE:
Martyn, Osborne, Sinnott, Southgate, Young, Thorn, Armstrong, Thomas, Bright, Salako, McGoldrick.
Subs: Humphrey (for Salako), Heald, Coleman.

Disaster for Dion Dublin on his full home début. In the forty-first minute he was carried off with a broken leg following a challenge by Eric Young. United showed they intended to fight all the way by once again grabbing a late winner. This time Mark Hughes was on target with a left-foot drive from a Brian McClair pass.

P	W	D	L	F	A	Pts	Psn
6	3	1	2	6	6	10	6

6 September | **OLD TRAFFORD** | 31,296

Manchester United (2) 2 **Kanchelskis (28)** **Bruce (44)**	**Leeds United (0) 0**
MANCHESTER UNITED: Schmeichel, Blackmore, Irwin, Bruce, Ferguson, Pallister, Kanchelskis, Ince, McClair, Hughes, Giggs. Subs: Martin, Wallace, Walsh.	LEEDS UNITED: Lukic, Newsome, Dorigo, Batty, Fairclough, Whyte, Cantona, Wallace, Chapman, McAllister, Speed. Subs: Strachan (for Wallace), Day, Hodge (for Newsome).

An outstanding performance from United who ran the champions ragged. And look who was playing for Leeds – Eric Cantona! Even the super Frenchman could do little to stop the Reds. Andrei Kanchelskis opened the scoring with a header from a Giggs cross, and just before half-time Steve Bruce made it 2–0 when Leeds failed to clear a corner.

P	W	D	L	F	A	Pts	Psn
7	4	1	2	8	6	13	4

12 September | **GOODISON PARK** | 30,002

Everton (0) 0	**Manchester United (1) 2** **McClair (29)** **Bruce (76 pen)**
EVERTON: Southall, Harper, Hinchcliffe, Ebbrell, Watson, Ablett, Warzycha, Beardsley, Johnston, Horne, Ward. Subs: Beagrie (for Ebbrell), Jackson, Kearton.	MANCHESTER UNITED: Schmeichel, Irwin, Blackmore, Bruce, Ferguson, Pallister, Kanchelskis, Ince, McClair, Hughes, Giggs. Subs: Martin, Wallace, Walsh.

Swift revenge for that defeat at Old Trafford. Brian McClair got his first goal of the season after Mark Hughes threaded a pass through the Everton defence, then Steve Bruce rammed home a penalty when Andrei Kanchelskis was brought down.

P	W	D	L	F	A	Pts	Psn
8	5	1	2	10	6	16	3

(*Inset*) Brian McClair just fails to make contact as Neil Ruddock of Tottenham slides in to take the ball. McClair was the first United player since George Best to score more than twenty League goals in a season when he netted twenty-four in 1987–88. In 1992–93 he scored nine championship goals even though he played most of his games in midfield. © *Action Images*

Player of the season Paul Ince forces his way through the Nottingham Forest defence, supported by Dion Dublin and Ryan Giggs, as Scot Gemmill tries to get in a challenge. © *Action Images*

Tottenham Hotspur (0) 1 **Durie (53)**	**Manchester United (1) 1** **Giggs (45)**
TOTTENHAM HOTSPUR: Walker, Austin, Van den Hauwe, Gray, Cundy, Ruddock, Sedgley, Durie, Turner, Sheringham, Allen. Subs: Hendry (for Gray), Thorsvedt, Tuttle (for Austin).	MANCHESTER UNITED: Schmeichel, Irwin, Blackmore, Bruce, Ferguson, Pallister, Kanchelskis, Ince, McClair, Hughes, Giggs. Subs: Martin, Walsh, Wallace (for Kanchelskis).

Ryan Giggs gave United the lead with a spectacular goal just before half-time and the Reds looked set to make it six wins in a row, but Tottenham equalized through Gordon Durie and managed to hold out against United's second-half pressure.

P	W	D	L	F	A	Pts	Psn
9	5	2	2	11	7	17	4

Manchester United (0) 0	**QPR (0) 0**
MANCHESTER UNITED: Schmeichel, Irwin, Blackmore, Bruce, Ferguson, Pallister, Kanchelskis, Ince, McClair, Hughes, Giggs. Subs: Martin, Walsh, Wallace (for Kanchelskis).	QPR: Stejskal, Bardsley, Brevett, Wilkins, Peacock, Maddix, Impey, Holloway, Ferdinand, Penrice, Sinton. Subs: Barker (for Ferdinand), Roberts, Channing.

Unbeaten in seven games. But home draws were United's downfall in their last campaign and this was an unwanted result. Fergie seemed worried about the lack of goals – two is the most they had managed to date – and speculation had it they were about to move for David Hirst till Sheffield Wednesday issued a 'hands off' warning.

P	W	D	L	F	A	Pts	Psn
10	5	3	2	11	7	18	4

Middlesbrough (0) 1
Slaven (59)

MIDDLESBROUGH:
Ironside, Morris, Phillips, Gittens, Whyte, Peake, Slaven, Mustoe, Wilkinson, Pollock, Wright.
Subs: Proctor, Pears, Hendrie (for Pollock).

Manchester United (1) 1
Bruce (44 pen)

MANCHESTER UNITED:
Schmeichel, Irwin, Phelan, Bruce, Ferguson, Pallister, Blackmore, Ince, McClair, Hughes, Giggs.
Subs: Robson (for Hughes), Walsh, Kanchelskis (for Phelan).

Bryan Robson's first taste of the Premier League. The United skipper made his return after having back trouble, but even he could do nothing to secure victory. Steve Bruce gave the Reds the lead thanks to a penalty after Denis Irwin was tripped, but 'Boro pulled back through Bernie Slaven.

P	W	D	L	F	A	Pts	Psn
11	5	4	2	12	8	19	6

Manchester United (0) 2
Hughes (78, 89)

MANCHESTER UNITED:
Schmeichel, Parker, Irwin, Bruce, Ferguson, Pallister, Kanchelskis, Ince, McClair, Hughes, Giggs.
Subs: Phelan, Walsh, Blackmore (for Kanchelskis).

Liverpool (2) 2
Hutchison (23)
Rush (44)

LIVERPOOL:
Grobbelaar, Marsh, Burrows, Nicol, Piechnik, Hutchison, Mcmanaman, Redknapp, Rush, Molby, Rosenthal.
Subs: Thomas (for Redknapp), James, Tanner (for Molby).

It looked as though the unbeaten run was over when Liverpool led 2–0 at half time. First Don Hutchison's low shot took a deflection past Schmeichel, then Ian Rush hit home a Rosenthal cross. Enter Mark Hughes and two brilliant goals. He lobbed Grobbelaar from a Blackmore pass, then with a minute to go, dived to head home from a Giggs cross. What an afternoon for the Welsh!

P	W	D	L	F	A	Pts	Psn
12	5	5	2	14	10	20	5

(*Below*) Fergie Mark II forces his way between Mike Marsh and Jan Molby of Liverpool as United push upfield at Old Trafford. Darren Ferguson, son of the United manager, played in fifteen Premier League games during the opening weeks of the season, but was then sidelined through injury. © *Action Images*

Bryan Robson in action against Aston Villa in the Premier League clash at Villa Park. The club skipper missed much of the 1992–93 season because of injury but returned as a steadying influence for the final run-in. © *Action Images*

24 October E W O O D P A R K **20,305**

Blackburn Rovers (0) 0

BLACKBURN ROVERS:
Mimms, May, Wright, Sherwood, Hendry, Moran,
Ripley, Cowans, Shearer, Newell, Wilcox.
Subs: Marker, Collier, Wegerle (for Ripley).

Manchester United (0) 0

MANCHESTER UNITED:
Schmeichel, Parker, Irwin, Bruce, Ferguson,
Pallister, Blackmore, Ince, McClair, Hughes,
Giggs.
Subs: Kanchelskis (for Ferguson), Walsh, Webb.

With Blackburn supporters claiming that this was to be their year of the championship, it was a game of great caution. Alan Shearer failed to impress, while at the other end Hughes, McClair and Giggs all had good chances. United's unbeaten run continued, but you don't win titles without winning games. Five successive draws was nothing to be proud of.

P	W	D	L	F	A	Pts	Psn
13	5	6	2	14	10	21	7

31 October O L D T R A F F O R D **32,622**

Manchester United (0) 0

MANCHESTER UNITED:
Schmeichel, Parker, Blackmore, Bruce, Ferguson,
Pallister, Kanchelskis, Ince, McClair, Hughes,
Giggs.
Subs: Robson (for Kanchelskis), Walsh, Phelan.

Wimbledon (0) 1
Sanchez (79)

WIMBLEDON:
Segers, Barton, Joseph, Jones, McLeary,
McAllister, Gibson, Earle, Holdsworth, Sanchez,
Dobbs.
Subs: Clarke (for Dobbs), Sullivan, Cotterill.

The run of draws ends . . . in defeat! Wimbledon, those well-known party spoilers, came to Old Trafford and stole three points on a night when football came second. Laurie Sanchez got the goal amid rumblings that Fergie would have to buy to end the goal famine. But who?

P	W	D	L	F	A	Pts	Psn
14	5	6	3	14	11	21	7

7 November VILLA PARK 39,063

Aston Villa (1) 1
Atkinson (12)

ASTON VILLA:
Spink, Barrett, Staunton, Teale, McGrath,
Richardson, Houghton, Parker, Saunders,
Atkinson, Small.
Subs: Yorke, Bosnich, Regis.

Manchester United (0) 0

MANCHESTER UNITED:
Schmeichel, Parker, Blackmore, Bruce, Ferguson,
Pallister, Robson, Ince, Sharpe, Hughes, Giggs.
Subs: McClair (for Ferguson), Digby, Kanchelskis.

Ten days after losing to Villa in the Coca-Cola Cup Ron Atkinson does it again. United just could not score against a Villa side, which seemed intent on making a firm challenge for the championship. Bryan Robson started his first game and Lee Sharpe was back from his long absence.

P	W	D	L	F	A	Pts	Psn
15	5	6	4	14	12	21	10

21 November OLD TRAFFORD 33,497

Manchester United (3) 3
McClair (10, 28)
Hughes (11)

MANCHESTER UNITED:
Schmeichel, Parker, Irwin, Bruce, Sharpe,
Pallister, Robson, Ince, McClair, Hughes, Giggs.
Subs: Phelan (for Irwin), Digby, Butt (for Ince).

Oldham Athletic (0) 0

OLDHAM ATHLETIC:
Hallworth, Halle, Pointon, Henry, Jobson,
Redmond, McDonald, Marshall, Sharp, Milligan,
Adams.
Subs: Olney, Gerrard, Bernard.

Victory at last and goals as well. United ran Oldham off their feet and it looked at one stage as if they could repeat the 6–2 thrashing of Boxing Day 1991. Brian McClair began it all when Hughes crossed from a parried Sharpe free kick, then a minute later Sparky was on target himself, running onto a McClair pass. Brian got his second when he forced the ball home following a clever Steve Bruce back-heel.

P	W	D	L	F	A	Pts	Psn
16	6	6	4	17	12	24	8

144

Old pals' act. Former United defender Mal Donaghy slides in to stop Mike Phelan at Stamford Bridge. Donaghy left for Chelsea in the summer of 1992 having joined United from Luton. Phelan played in just eleven Premier League fixtures during a season in which he was plagued by injury.
© *Action Images*

28 November　　　　　　　　　　**H I G H B U R Y**　　　　　　　　　　29,739

Arsenal (0) 0

ARSENAL:
Seaman, Dixon, Morrow, Hillier, Bould, Adams,
Jensen, Wright, Campbell, Merson, Limpar.
Subs: Parlour (for Jensen), Millar, Flatts.

Manchester United (1) 1
Hughes (27)

MANCHESTER UNITED:
Schmeichel, Parker, Irwin, Bruce, Sharpe,
Pallister, Robson, Ince, McClair, Hughes, Giggs.
Subs: Kanchelskis, Digby, Phelan.

Enter Eric Cantona! Two days before the game
Fergie pulled off the coup of the season by signing
the French star from Leeds. Eric was a spectator
after being registered too late to play but he saw

Mark Hughes ram the winner home after Ryan
Giggs hit the post from a Lee Sharpe cross. What lay
ahead? Only time would tell.

P	W	D	L	F	A	Pts	Psn
17	7	6	4	18	12	27	5

6 December　　　　　　　　**O L D　T R A F F O R D**　　　　　　　　35,408

Manchester United (1) 2
Ince (20)
Hughes (73)

MANCHESTER UNITED:
Schmeichel, Parker, Irwin, Bruce, Sharpe,
Pallister, Robson, Ince, McClair, Hughes, Giggs.
Subs: Cantona (for Giggs), Digby, M. Phelan.

Manchester City (0) 1
Quinn (74)

MANCHESTER CITY:
Coton, Brightwell, T. Phelan, McMahon, Curle,
Hill, White, Sheron, Quinn, Simpson, Holden.
Subs: Reid (for Simpson), Margetson, Flitcroft
(for Sheron).

A great performance from United, but it almost
turned sour. Two great goals, first a Paul Ince shot
from 20 yards, then a Mark Hughes volley in the
second half seemed to tie it up. But City rallied as

United tired and an injury to Steve Bruce was the
key. Niall Quinn scored after David White collided
with Bruce and United had to hang on until the
whistle.

P	W	D	L	F	A	Pts	Psn
18	8	6	4	20	13	30	5

OLD TRAFFORD

Manchester United (0) 1
Hughes (59)

MANCHESTER UNITED:
Schmeichel, Parker, Irwin, Bruce, Sharpe,
Pallister, Cantona, Ince, McClair, Hughes, Giggs.
Subs: Kanchelskis, Digby, Blackmore.

Norwich City (0) 0

NORWICH CITY:
Gunn, Culverhouse, Bowen, Butterworth, Polston,
Sutch, Crook, Beckford, Robins, Fox, Phillips.
Subs: Sutton (for Beckford), Marshall, Megson (for
Crook).

Eric the Red makes his home début. The vision of Cantona was obvious from the start as he got his team-mates clicking. This was supposed to be the day when Mark Robins came back to Old Trafford to haunt Alex Ferguson. Far from it. Robins had one shot on target, Mark Hughes grabbed the winner and the high-flying Canaries had their wings clipped.

P	W	D	L	F	A	Pts	Psn
19	9	6	4	21	13	33	3

STAMFORD BRIDGE

Chelsea (0) 1
Lee (67)

CHELSEA:
Hitchcock, Hall, Sinclair, Townsend, Lee,
Donaghy, Stuart, Fleck, Le Saux, Newton, Wise.
Subs: Burley, Colgan, Harford (for Fleck).

Manchester United (0) 1
Cantona (71)

MANCHESTER UNITED:
Schmeichel, Parker, Irwin, Bruce, Phelan,
Pallister, Cantona, Ince, McClair, Hughes,
Sharpe.
Subs: Kanchelskis (for Phelan), Digby,
Blackmore.

Ooh, aah Cantona! Eric starts to pay back his transfer fee. The Frenchman got his first goal for United on a mud heap of a pitch, in a far from inspiring game, but the draw kept United on a roll. Chelsea went ahead through David Lee's powerful free kick, and four minutes later Eric struck, spinning on the ball before shooting low following a Michael Phelan headed pass from a Lee Sharpe cross.

P	W	D	L	F	A	Pts	Psn
20	9	7	4	22	14	34	4

Denis Irwin found his niche at left full back in the championship side. His powerful free kicks added to United's goal power and five times during the season he scored crucial goals. And he had something to celebrate after scoring the second against Tottenham in the 4–1 victory at Old Trafford. © *Action Images*

(*Below*) Sheffield Wednesday's John Sheridan is a self-confessed United supporter having watched the Reds from the Stretford End when he was a teenager. As for Paul Ince he held off all challengers during 1993 not only establishing himself in the United line-up but staking a claim for a regular England place as well. © *Action Images*

26 December   **HILLSBOROUGH**   37,708

Sheffield Wednesday (2) 3
Hirst (3), Bright (7), Sheridan (62)

SHEFFIELD WEDNESDAY:
Woods, Nilsson, Worthington, Palmer, Anderson,
Shirtliff, Wilson, Waddle, Hirst, Bright, Sheridan.
Subs: Bart-Williams, Pressman, Harkes.

Manchester United (0) 3
McClair (68, 81), Cantona (84)

MANCHESTER UNITED:
Schmeichel, Parker, Irwin, Bruce, Sharpe,
Pallister, Cantona, Ince, McClair, Hughes, Giggs.
Subs: Kanchelskis (for Giggs), Digby, Phelan.

The halfway stage in the season and if there are any more games like this the fans will be fighting to get in. It looked as though the Christmas pudding had taken its toll as the Reds trailed 3–0 through Hirst, Bright and Sheridan. But United had never been out of the game and stormed back. Brian McClair scored twice, first running in at Chris Woods' far post, then with a near-post header, both from Lee Sharpe crosses. Lee did it again in the eighty-fourth minute and laid on the equalizer for that man Cantona . . . 3–3. Phew!

P	W	D	L	F	A	Pts	Psn
21	9	8	4	25	17	35	3

28 December   **OLD TRAFFORD**   36,025

Manchester United (2) 5
Giggs (6), Hughes (41), Cantona (65 pen)
Sharpe (78), Irwin (83)

MANCHESTER UNITED:
Schmeichel, Parker, Irwin, Bruce, Sharpe,
Pallister, Cantona, Ince, McClair, Hughes, Giggs.
Subs: Kanchelskis (for Giggs), Digby, Phelan (for
Bruce).

Coventry City (0) 0

COVENTRY CITY:
Gould, Borrows, Babb, Atherton, Sansom,
Williams, McGrath, Hurst, Rosario, Quinn,
Gallacher.
Subs: Pearce, Ogrizovic, Ndlovu (for Williams).

It had to happen some time. United had been threatening to run riot and this time they did. Coventry never stood a chance against the onslaught. Giggs chipped the first, cutting in from the right. Hughes stabbed home number two after a flowing McClair, Giggs, Cantona move. Eric himself stroked home a penalty when Parker's cross was handled. Sharpe got his first of the season even though he mishit the shot. Then finally Denis Irwin almost lifted the net off with a fierce drive.

P	W	D	L	F	A	Pts	Psn
22	10	8	4	30	17	38	2

9 January   **OLD TRAFFORD**   **35,648**

Manchester United (1) 4
Cantona (40), Irwin (52),
McClair (53), Parker (58)

MANCHESTER UNITED:
Schmeichel, Parker, Irwin, Bruce, Sharpe,
Pallister, Cantona, Ince, McClair, Hughes, Giggs.
Subs: Kanchelskis (for Giggs), Sealey, Phelan
(for Ince).

Tottenham Hotspur (0) 1
Barmby (87)

TOTTENHAM HOTSPUR:
Thorsvedt, Austin, Edinburgh, Samways, Mabbutt,
Ruddock, Howells, Barmby, Nayim, Sheringham,
Allen.
Subs: Bergsson (for Austin), Walker, Anderton
(for Nayim).

Spurs felt the full power of the rampant Reds. Cantona opened with a looping header from an Irwin cross helped on by Sharpe. Irwin shot low from Cantona's pass for the second. McClair hit the third from way out, and finally Paul Parker got his first goal for United after a one-two with McClair.

P	W	D	L	F	A	Pts	Psn
23	11	8	4	34	18	41	1

18 January   **LOFTUS ROAD**   **21,117**

QPR (1) 1
Allen (43)

QPR:
Roberts, Bardsley, Wilson, Barker, Peacock,
McDonald, Impey, Holloway, Bailey, Allen, Sinton.
Subs: Thompson (for Peacock), Stejskal, Brevett.

Manchester United (2) 3
Ince (26), Giggs (30), Kanchelskis (48)

MANCHESTER UNITED:
Schmeichel, Parker, Irwin, Bruce, Sharpe,
Pallister, Kanchelskis, Ince, McClair, Hughes,
Giggs.
Subs : Phelan (for Hughes), Sealey, Lawton.

Remember New Year's Day 1992: United 1 QPR 4? Nobody would let Fergie forget that scoreline as this fixture loomed. But it was a thing of the past as United kept up their run at Loftus Road. Paul Ince's overhead kick from Sharpe's cross started it off. Ryan Giggs chipped the 'keeper from an Irwin through ball, then Andrei Kanchelskis fired home the third, as play switched wings in a Sharpe–Giggs–Kanchelskis move.

P	W	D	L	F	A	Pts	Psn
24	12	8	4	37	19	44	1

Neil Webb's career at Old Trafford was hit by injury
after only a few weeks when he ruptured an
Achilles' tendon while on England duty in Sweden
in 1989. Four years later he was sold back to
Nottingham Forest, returning to Old Trafford in a
side destined for relegation. Goals from Paul Ince
(pictured) and Mark Hughes gave United the
points. © *Empics/Steve Etherington*

(*Below*) *Clockwise*: Brian McClair, Mark Hughes,
Lee Sharpe and Eric Cantona surround a grounded
Ryan Giggs as they celebrate his second goal
against Southampton, a strike which gave United a
2–1 win at Old Trafford and kept them hot on the
heels of Aston Villa. © *Action Images*

27 January   **O L D   T R A F F O R D**   **36,085**

Manchester United (0) 2	Nottingham Forest (0) 0
Ince (48), Hughes (68)	
MANCHESTER UNITED:	NOTTINGHAM FOREST:
Schmeichel, Parker, Irwin, Bruce, Sharpe,	Crossley, Laws, Williams, Chettle, Tiler, Keane,
Pallister, Cantona, Ince, McClair, Hughes, Giggs.	Bannister, Gemmill, Clough, Webb, Woan.
Subs: Kanchelskis, Sealey, Phelan.	Subs: Crosby (for Woan), Marriott, Orlygsson.

The return of Neil Webb, but like Mark Robins, the United old boy was on the losing side. Forest were struggling to survive in the Premier League, but played football all the way. Paul Ince's third goal of the season was a 25-yard rocket which took a deflection, then Mark Hughes rammed home his twelfth from a Cantona lob.

P	W	D	L	F	A	Pts	Psn
25	13	8	4	39	19	47	1

30 January   **P O R T M A N   R O A D**   **22,068**

Ipswich Town (1) 2	Manchester United (0) 1
Kiwomya (20), Yallop (48)	**McClair (84)**
IPSWICH TOWN:	MANCHESTER UNITED:
Baker, Johnson, Thompson, Williams, Whelan,	Schmeichel, Parker, Irwin, Bruce, Sharpe,
Linnighan, Yallop, Guentchev, Bozinoski, Dozzell,	Pallister, Cantona, Ince, McClair, Hughes, Giggs.
Kiwomya.	Subs: Kanchelskis (for Sharpe), Sealey, Phelan.
Subs: Wark (for Bozinoski), Forrest, Stockwell (for	
Guentchev).	

All good things come to an end. After a run of ten League games without defeat, things went wrong against a side which was threatening the pace-setters. Kiwomya's opener was a gift after Peter Schmeichel missed a clearance when the ball bobbled on the bumpy pitch. Yallop hit a wallop of a shot after a break from defence. McClair scrambled one home with six minutes to go and the Reds came close to equalizing, but Ipswich held out.

P	W	D	L	F	A	Pts	Psn
26	13	8	5	40	21	47	2

6 February OLD TRAFFORD **36,156**

Manchester United (0) 2	Sheffield United (1) 1
McClair (64)	Carr (7)
Cantona (80)	

MANCHESTER UNITED:	SHEFFIELD UNITED:
Schmeichel, Parker, Irwin, Bruce, Sharpe, Pallister, Cantona, Ince, McClair, Hughes, Giggs. Subs: Kanchelskis (for Giggs), Sealey, Phelan.	Kelly, Ward, Cowan, Hoyland, Gayle, Beesley, Carr, Kamara, Bryson, Deane, Hartfield. Subs: Cork (for Bryson), Kite, Bradshaw (for Kamara).

United got the show back on the road again, but not before Franz Carr scared them into action. He put the Blades ahead after a long clearance. Eric Cantona headed down and Brian McClair rammed home the equalizer, then with only ten minutes to go the ball was sliced to Cantona by a defender and he struck the winner.

P	W	D	L	F	A	Pts	Psn
27	14	8	5	42	22	50	1

8 February ELLAND ROAD **34,166**

Leeds United (0) 0	Manchester United (0) 0

LEEDS UNITED:	MANCHESTER UNITED:
Lukic, Sellars, Dorigo, Batty, Newsome, Whyte, Bowman, Shutt, Chapman, McAllister, Speed. Subs: Strandli (for Shutt), Day, Hodge (for Sellars).	Schmeichel, Parker, Irwin, Bruce, Sharpe, Pallister, Cantona, Ince, McClair, Hughes, Giggs. Subs: Kanchelskis (for Giggs), Sealey, Phelan.

Eric Cantona would not have won a popularity poll amongst the Leeds supporters. United held out as the home side fought for survival after an amazing slip down the table. The point was worth more to the reigning champions than it was to Fergie's boys.

P	W	D	L	F	A	Pts	Psn
28	14	9	5	42	22	51	1

Great defending from the long-legged Gary Pallister as he forces the ball away from Dean Saunders the Aston Villa striker in the game at Old Trafford. It was a goal from Saunders, the former Liverpool star, which knocked United out of the Coca Cola Cup in an earlier clash at Villa Park, a result seen by Bryan Robson as vital to United's title hopes. 'It freed us for a run at the championship without the backlog of fixtures cup success can cause.' © *Action Images*

(*Below*) Liverpool 'keeper David James is rooted to the spot as Mark Hughes heads United into the lead three minutes before half-time. The biggest crowd of the season, 44,574, saw United pick up three points at Anfield. © *Action Images*

20 February	OLD TRAFFORD	36,257

Manchester United (0) 2 **Giggs (82, 83)**	**Southampton (0) 1** **Banger (77)**
MANCHESTER UNITED: Schmeichel, Parker, Irwin, Bruce, Sharpe, Pallister, Cantona, Ince, McClair, Hughes, Giggs. Subs: Kanchelskis, Sealey, Phelan.	SOUTHAMPTON: Flowers, Kenna, Adams, Widdrington, Hall, Monkou, Le Tissier, Dodd, Dowie, Maddison, Benali. Subs: Banger (for Le Tissier), Andrews, Moore.

Another tricky one with Nicky Banger scoring first for Saints. United slipped off the top even though they won, but they had a game in hand on leaders Aston Villa. It was Ryan Giggs with two late goals who saved United's blushes. His first was made by Cantona's pass, his second thanks to Hughes heading down as Giggs raced forward.

P	W	D	L	F	A	Pts	Psn
29	15	9	5	44	23	54	2

27 February	OLD TRAFFORD	36,251

Manchester United (1) 3 **Giggs (21)** **Irwin (79)** **Cantona (85)**	**Middlesbrough (0) 0**
MANCHESTER UNITED: Schmeichel, Parker, Irwin, Bruce, Sharpe, Pallister, Cantona, Ince, McClair, Hughes, Giggs. Subs: Kanchelskis, Sealey, Phelan.	MIDDLESBROUGH: Pears, Morris, Phillips, White, Mohan, Peake, Hendrie, Mustoe, Wilkinson, Kamara, Wright. Subs: Slaven (for Mustoe), Ironside, Kernaghan.

Middlesbrough goalkeeper Stephen Pears began his career with United and he wooed the home fans with an incredible display which kept United down to three. Giggs netted the first from the narrowest of angles; Irwin bent a free kick round the 'Boro wall; and Cantona kept on running after his first shot was blocked and grabbed the third.

P	W	D	L	F	A	Pts	Psn
30	16	9	5	47	23	57	2

6 March ANFIELD 44,574

Liverpool (0) 1
Rush (50)

LIVERPOOL:
James, Redknapp, Jones, Nicol, Wright,
Bjornebye, Mcmanaman, Hutchison, Walters,
Barnes, Stewart.
Subs: Burrows (for Walters), Hooper, Rush
(for Stewart).

Manchester United (1) 2
Hughes (42)
McClair (55)

MANCHESTER UNITED:
Schmeichel, Parker, Irwin, Bruce, Sharpe,
Pallister, Kanchelskis, Ince, McClair, Hughes,
Giggs.
Subs: Dublin, Sealey, Phelan.

Anfield, where better to go back to the top. Electrifying United never looked like losing. Liverpool needed the points to keep away from the relegation zone! Mark Hughes put the Reds in front with a flying header. Ian Rush rubbed it out with a superb volley from the right. But when Brian McClair headed down a Pallister flick-on from a Sharpe corner it was all over.

P	W	D	L	F	A	Pts	Psn
31	17	9	5	49	24	60	1

9 March BOUNDARY PARK 17,106

Oldham Athletic (1) 1
Adams (25)

OLDHAM ATHLETIC:
Gerrard, Halle, Pointon, Henry, Jobson, Fleming,
Adams, Bernard, Olney, Milligan, Brennan.
Subs: Palmer, Keeley, Redmond (for Pointon).

Manchester United (0) 0

MANCHESTER UNITED:
Schmeichel, Parker, Irwin, Bruce, Sharpe,
Pallister, Kanchelskis, Ince, McClair, Hughes,
Giggs.
Subs: Dublin (for Kanchelskis), Sealey, Phelan.

United took one look at the Oldham pitch and that seemed to be that. Latics took the lead through a far-post header from Neil Adams, the smallest player on the field, and held out under siege for over an hour. Oldham may well have stayed up because of the win as it inspired them to a tremendous fight against relegation. It was United's last defeat of the season.

P	W	D	L	F	A	Pts	Psn
32	17	9	6	49	25	60	1

A spectacular effort from Lee Sharpe as he tries to crack the Coventry defence at Highfield Road. He was unlucky here but was on target against Coventry in the 5–0 win at Old Trafford scoring his only goal of the season. © Empics/Phil O'Brien

14 March   O L D   T R A F F O R D   36,163

Manchester United (0) 1
Hughes (57)

MANCHESTER UNITED:
Schmeichel, Parker, Irwin, Bruce, Sharpe,
Pallister, Cantona, Ince, McClair, Hughes, Giggs.
Subs: Robson, Sealey, Kanchelskis.

Aston Villa (0) 1
Staunton (52)

ASTON VILLA:
Bosnich, Barrett, Staunton, Teale, McGrath,
Richardson, Houghton, Parker, Saunders, Yorke,
Small.
Subs: Cox, Spink, Daley (for Parker).

What a cracker this was. Villa took the lead through an amazing shot from Steve Staunton, but United dominated for long periods and the equalizer was no surprise. It came just five minutes later when Mark Hughes headed home powerfully following an Irwin cross to Cantona.

P	W	D	L	F	A	Pts	Psn
33	17	10	6	50	26	61	1

20 March   M A I N E   R O A D   37,136

Manchester City (0) 1
Quinn (58)

MANCHESTER CITY:
Coton, Hill, Phelan, Reid, Curle, Vonk, White,
Sheron, Quinn, Flitcroft, Holden.
Subs: Quigley, Margetson, Ingebrigsten.

Manchester United (0) 1
Cantona (68)

MANCHESTER UNITED:
Schmeichel, Parker, Irwin, Bruce, Sharpe,
Pallister, Cantona, Ince, McClair, Hughes, Giggs.
Subs: Robson, Sealey, Kanchelskis.

City would have liked nothing better than to stop United's championship challenge, but Eric Cantona cut short their celebrations when he headed home from a Lee Sharpe cross. This was after Niall Quinn had been given a free header from a Holden cross when Pallister was injured.

P	W	D	L	F	A	Pts	Psn
34	17	11	6	51	27	62	1

24 March   **OLD TRAFFORD**   **37,301**

Manchester United (0) 0

MANCHESTER UNITED:
Schmeichel, Parker, Irwin, Bruce, Sharpe,
Pallister, Cantona, Ince, McClair, Hughes, Giggs.
Subs: Robson (for Hughes), Sealey, Kanchelskis.

Arsenal (0) 0

ARSENAL:
Seaman, Dixon, Keown, Morrow, Linighan,
Adams, Jensen, Wright, Campbell, Merson,
Carter.
Subs: Hillier (for Adams), Millar, Parlour
(for Carter).

A good solid display by Arsenal who held out against everything United could muster. Both sides came close to scoring and in the end a draw was a fair result. The Reds slipped down the League as Norwich came back into contention . . . and they were next.

P	W	D	L	F	A	Pts	Psn
35	17	12	6	51	27	63	3

5 April   **CARROW ROAD**   **20,582**

Norwich City (0) 1
Robins (60)

NORWICH CITY:
Gunn, Culverhouse, Bowen, Sutton, Polston,
Megson, Crook, Goss, Robins, Fox, Phillips.
Subs: Power, Walton, Ekuko (for Megson).

Manchester United (3) 3
Giggs (13), Kanchelskis (19)
Cantona (21)

MANCHESTER UNITED:
Schmeichel, Parker, Irwin, Bruce, Sharpe,
Pallister, Cantona, Ince, McClair, Kanchelskis,
Giggs.
Subs: Robson (for Kanchelskis), Sealey, Dublin.

It was billed as the championship decider, and as far as Norwich were concerned, it was. United were magnificent, tearing into the Canaries from the start. The speed of Giggs, Kanchelskis and Sharpe was too much for the home side. The first goal came when Cantona lifted the ball over the defence and Giggs weaved his way through. Six minutes later Andrei Kanchelskis sprinted in from the right wing and shot low, and two minutes later Eric Cantona sealed it from an Ince run and pass. Mark Robins got a second half consolation goal from a Ruel Fox cross.

P	W	D	L	F	A	Pts	Psn
36	18	12	6	54	28	66	2

Steve Clarke the Chelsea full back earns himself an unwanted place in the record books as he pushes the ball out of the reach of his own goalkeeper Dave Beasant. The own goal gave United a 2–0 half time lead with Eric Cantona sealing things in the second period. © *Action Images*

(*Below*) The ups and downs of football. Paul Parker out jumps Crystal Palace's Simon Osborne as United push for victory at Selhurst Park. It was a game which virtually secured the title because as United won 2–0 rivals Aston Villa lost 3–0 at Blackburn. The result also put Palace in deep trouble and eventually they were relegated and manager Steve Coppell resigned. © *Action Images*

Manchester United (0) 2
Bruce (86, 90)

MANCHESTER UNITED:
Schmeichel, Parker, Irwin, Bruce, Sharpe,
Pallister, Cantona, Ince, McClair, Hughes, Giggs.
Subs: Robson (for Parker), Sealey, Phelan.

Sheffield Wednesday (0) 1
Sheridan [pen] (65)

SHEFFIELD WEDNESDAY:
Woods, Nilsson, Worthington, Palmer, Sheridan,
Anderson, Wilson, Waddle, King, Jemson,
Watson.
Subs: Bright (for Jemson), Bart-Williams
(for Wilson), Pressman.

Old Trafford's match of the season and one which played a vital part in the title race. For the first hour it was frustrating for United's supporters as Wednesday wasted time. Then referee Michael Peck pulled a muscle and was replaced by linesman John Hilditch. Within minutes he awarded a penalty and Wednesday went ahead through John Sheridan. With six minutes to go Steve Bruce rose to head in a Denis Irwin corner, and in the sixth minute of added time did the same again from a Gary Pallister flick, and they still played another minute. But United were back on top.

P	W	D	L	F	A	Pts	Psn
37	19	12	6	56	29	69	1

Coventry City (0) 0

COVENTRY CITY:
Gould, Borrows, Babb, Atherton, Gynn, Rennie,
McGrath, Hurst, Quinn, Wegerle, Williams.
Subs: Busst, Ogrizovic, Jenkinson (for McGrath).

Manchester United (1) 1
Irwin (40)

MANCHESTER UNITED:
Schmeichel, Parker, Irwin, Bruce, Sharpe,
Pallister, Cantona, Ince, McClair, Hughes, Giggs.
Subs: Robson (for Cantona), Sealey, Phelan.

One shot all afternoon and three points. Denis Irwin's goal in the fortieth minute was enough to beat a resilient Coventry, who had Mick Quinn sent off two minutes before the final whistle.

P	W	D	L	F	A	Pts	Psn
38	20	12	6	57	29	72	1

17 April   OLD TRAFFORD   40,139

Manchester United (2) 3
Hughes (24), Clarke o.g. (45), Cantona (48)

MANCHESTER UNITED:
Schmeichel, Parker, Irwin, Bruce, Sharpe,
Pallister, Cantona, Ince, McClair, Hughes, Giggs.
Subs: Robson (for McClair), Kanchelskis (for
Giggs), Sealey.

Chelsea (0) 0

CHELSEA:
Beasant, Clarke, Sinclair, Townsend, Johnsen,
Donaghy, Stuart, Spencer, Shipperley, Hall, Wise.
Subs: Barnard (for Donaghy), Kharine,
Livingstone (for Shipperley).

Never a classic but another vital victory. Chelsea had been United's Old Trafford 'bogey' side for years, but not this time. Sharpe won the ball on the right to set up Mark Hughes for a near-post shot.

The unfortunate Steve Clarke headed into his own net just on half-time – again from a Sharpe cross – then Eric Cantona headed in a Giggs chip for his ninth United goal.

P	W	D	L	F	A	Pts	Psn
39	21	12	6	60	29	75	1

21 April   SELHURST PARK   30,115

Crystal Palace (0) 0

CRYSTAL PALACE:
Martyn, Shaw, Southgate, Coleman, Young,
Thorn, Humphrey, Newman, Armstrong, Osborne,
McGoldrick.
Subs: Williams, Woodman, Ndah (for Osborne).

Manchester United (0) 2
Hughes (64), Ince (88)

MANCHESTER UNITED:
Schmeichel, Parker, Irwin, Bruce, Kanchelskis,
Pallister, Cantona, Ince, McClair, Hughes, Giggs.
Subs: Robson (for Kanchelskis), Sealey, Phelan.

The night United won the championship. Forget what the record books say, this was the game when they did it, as Aston Villa were hammered 3–0 at Blackburn. The Reds staged a tremendous fight in the second half with Paul Ince an inspiration. Mark

Hughes smashed home a Cantona cross for the first, Ince ran at the defence and shot across goal for the second. United were four points clear and the celebrations started.

P	W	D	L	F	A	Pts	Psn
40	22	12	6	62	29	78	1

The champions take the lead against Wimbledon in the closing match of the season. Paul Ince smashes home a fierce shot for his sixth of the campaign as United open up a ten-point gap over second-placed Aston Villa. © *Action Images*

3 May   **OLD TRAFFORD**   **40,447**

Manchester United (1) 3
Giggs (22), Ince (61), Pallister (89)

MANCHESTER UNITED:
Schmeichel, Parker, Irwin, Bruce, Sharpe,
Pallister, Cantona, Ince, McClair, Hughes, Giggs.
Subs: Robson (for Sharpe), Sealey, Kanchelskis
(for McClair).

Blackburn Rovers (1) 1
Gallacher (8)

BLACKBURN ROVERS:
Mimms, Marker, Le Saux, Sherwood, Hendry,
Moran, Ripley, Atkins, Gallacher, Newell, Wilcox.
Subs: Cowans (for Moran), Talia, Anderson.

Champions! Oldham had beaten Villa the previous day and no-one could stop United now. But they wanted to do it in style and proved worthy winners against Blackburn with an amazing fightback after Rovers stole the lead early on through Kevin Gallacher. Giggs bent a free kick round the wall to equalize, Cantona set Ince up for the second and, with a minute left, Gary Pallister got his first goal of the season from another free kick on the edge of the box.

P	W	D	L	F	A	Pts	Psn
41	23	12	6	65	30	81	1

9 May   **SELHURST PARK**   **30,115**

Wimbledon (0) 1
Holdsworth (82)

WIMBLEDON:
Segers, Barton, McAllister, Jones, Scales,
Fitzgerald, Ardley, Earle, Fashanu, Holdsworth,
Clarke.
Subs: Sanchez, Kee, Joseph (for Ardley).

Manchester United (0) 2
Ince (62)
Robson (75)

MANCHESTER UNITED:
Schmeichel, Parker, Irwin, Bruce, Sharpe,
Pallister, Robson, Ince, McClair, Hughes,
Cantona.
Subs: Giggs (for Irwin) Sealey, Dublin.

After a week as champions, United and their fans are still riding on cloud nine. Selhurst Park has seen nothing like it. Wimbledon were outnumbered, outshouted and outplayed. The Reds took the lead through man-of-the-season Paul Ince after a corner was half cleared, then Bryan Robson with his first Premier League goal, brought the curtain down on a wonderful season.

P	W	D	L	F	A	Pts	Psn
42	24	12	6	67	31	84	1

The run of seven consecutive wins which secured the championship was the key point of the season. Compare these two charts which show the progress of United in 1992 and 1993.

SEASON 1991–92

	Date	Ven	Opponents	Result		L/p	Pts
	August						
1	17	H	Notts County	2–0	W		3
2	21	A	Aston Villa	1–0	W		6
3	24	A	Everton	0–0	D		7
4	28	H	Oldham Ath.	1–0	W	1	10
5	31	H	Leeds Utd	1–1	D	1	11
	Sept						
6	3	A	Wimbledon	2–1	W	1	14
7	7	H	Norwich City	3–0	W	1	17
8	14	A	Southampton	1–0	W	1	20
9	21	H	Luton	5–0	W	1	23
10	28	A	Tottenham H.	2–1	W	1	26
	Oct						
11	6	H	Liverpool	0–0	D	1	27
12	19	H	Arsenal	1–1	D	1	28
13	26	A	Sheff. Wed.	2–3	L	2	28
	Nov						
14	2	H	Sheff. Utd	2–0	W	1	31
15	16	A	Man. City	0–0	D	2	32
16	23	H	West Ham	2–1	W	1	35
17	30	A	Crystal Pal.	3–1	W	2	38
	Dec						
18	7	H	Coventry	4–0	W	2	41
19	15	A	Chelsea	3–1	W	1	44
20	26	A	Oldham Ath.	6–3	W	1	47
21	29	A	Leeds Utd	1–1	D	1	48
	Jan						
22	1	H	QPR	1–4	L	2	48
23	11	H	Everton	1–0	W	1	51
24	18	A	Notts County	1–1	D	2	52
25	22	H	Aston Villa	1–0	W	1	55
	Feb						
26	1	A	Arsenal	1–1	D	2	56
27	8	H	Sheff. Wed.	1–1	D	1	57
28	22	H	Crystal Pal.	2–0	W	1	60
29	26	H	Chelsea	1–1	D	1	61
30	29	A	Coventry	0–0	D	1	62
	Mar						
31	14	A	Sheff. Utd	2–1	W	2	65
32	18	A	Nottm Forest	0–1	L	2	65
33	21	H	Wimbledon	0–0	D	2	66
34	28	A	QPR	0–0	D	2	67
35	31	A	Norwich	3–1	W	1	70
	Apr						
36	7	H	Man. City	1–1	D	1	71
37	16	H	Southampton	1–0	W	1	74
38	18	A	Luton	1–1	D	1	75
39	20	H	Nottm Forest	1–2	L	2	75
40	22	A	West Ham	0–1	L	2	75
41	26	A	Liverpool	0–2	L	2	75
	May						
42	5	H	Tottenham H.	3–1	W	2	78

SEASON 1992–93

	Date	Ven	Opponents	Result		L/p	Pts
	August						
1	15	A	Sheff. Utd	1–2	L		0
2	19	H	Everton	0–3	L		0
3	22	H	Ipswich	1–1	D		1
4	24	A	Southampton	1–0	W		4
5	29	A	Nottm Forest	2–0	W	8	7
	Sept						
6	2	H	Crystal Pal.	1–0	W	6	10
7	6	H	Leeds Utd	2–0	W	4	13
8	12	A	Everton	2–0	W	3	16
9	19	A	Tottenham H.	1–1	D	4	17
10	26	H	QPR	0–0	D	4	18
	Oct						
11	3	A	Middlesbro'	1–1	D	6	19
12	18	H	Liverpool	2–2	D	5	20
13	24	A	Blackburn	0–0	D	7	21
14	31	H	Wimbledon	0–1	L	7	21
	Nov						
15	7	A	Aston Villa	0–1	L	10	21
16	21	H	Oldham Ath	3–0	W	8	24
17	28	A	Arsenal	1–0	W	5	27
	Dec						
18	6	H	Man. City	2–1	W	5	30
19	12	H	Norwich City	1–0	W	3	33
20	19	A	Chelsea	1–1	D	4	34
21	26	A	Sheff. Wed.	3–3	D	3	35
22	28	H	Coventry	5–0	W	2	38
	Jan						
23	9	H	Tottenham H.	4–1	W	1	41
24	18	A	QPR	3–1	W	1	44
25	27	H	Nottm Forest	2–0	W	1	47
26	30	A	Ipswich	1–2	L	2	47
	Feb						
27	6	H	Sheff. Utd	2–1	W	1	50
28	8	A	Leeds Utd	0–0	D	1	51
29	20	H	Southampton	2–1	W	2	54
30	27	H	Middlesbro'	3–0	W	2	57
	Mar						
31	6	A	Liverpool	2–1	W	1	60
32	9	A	Oldham Ath.	0–1	L	1	60
33	14	H	Aston Villa	1–1	D	1	61
34	20	A	Man. City	1–1	D	2	62
35	24	H	Arsenal	0–0	D	3	63
	Apr						
36	5	A	Norwich City	3–1	W	2	66
37	10	H	Sheff. Wed.	2–1	W	1	69
38	12	A	Coventry	1–0	W	1	72
39	17	H	Chelsea	3–0	W	1	75
40	21	A	Crystal Pal.	2–0	W	1	78
	May						
41	3	H	Blackburn	3–1	W	1	81
42	9	A	Wimbledon	2–1	W	1	84

APPEARANCES

	Lge	FA	LC	UEFA	Sub
Schmeichel	42	3	2	1	–
Irwin	40	3	3	2	–
Blackmore	12	–	1	1	3
Bruce	42	3	3	2	–
Pallister	42	3	3	2	–
Ferguson	15	–	1	–	–
Kanchelskis	14	1	2	1	12
Ince	41	2	3	1	–
McClair	41	3	3	2	1
Hughes	41	2	3	2	–
Giggs	40	2	2	1	1
Robson	5	–	1	–	11
Parker	31	3	2	–	1
Sharpe	27	3	–	–	–
Cantona	21	1	–	–	1
Phelan	5	2	–	1	6
Dublin	3	–	–	–	4
Webb (now Nottm For)	–	–	1	2	1
Walsh	–	–	1	1	–
Martin	–	–	1	1	–
Wallace	–	1	1	2	2
Neville	–	–	–	–	1
Beckham	–	–	–	–	1
Butt	–	–	–	–	1
Gillespie	–	1	–	–	1

(unused substitutes are not included)

GOAL SCORERS 1992–93

	Lge	FA	LC	UEFA
Hughes	15	–	1	–
McClair	9	–	–	–
Giggs	9	2	–	–
Cantona*	9	–	–	–
Ince	6	–	–	–
Bruce	5	–	–	–
Irwin	5	–	–	–
Kanchelskis	3	–	–	–
Dublin	1	–	–	–
Sharpe	1	–	–	–
Parker	1	–	–	–
Pallister	1	–	–	–
Robson	1	–	–	–
Wallace	–	–	1	–
Phelan	–	1	–	–
Gillespie	–	1	–	–
Own goal	1	–	–	–

(*also scored 8 goals with Leeds Utd)